Also from Aplomb Publishing

Reel Horror - True Horrors Behind Hollywood's Scary Movies

Master of Disaster: Irwin Allen - The Disaster Years

Curse of the Silver Screen - Tragedy & Disaster Behind the Movies

Disaster in the Sky - Behind the Scenes of the Airport Movies

Alfred Hitchcock: The Icon Years

www.aplombpublishing.com

Disaster on Film
A Behind the Scenes Look at Hollywood Disaster Movies

by John William Law

Disaster on Film - A Behind the Scenes Look at Hollywood Disaster Movies.

Published by Aplomb Publishing, San Francisco, CA.
Copyright 2010.

ISBN 978-09825195-9-2
Manufactured in the United States of America

Dedicated to disaster movie lovers everywhere.

table of contents
Behind the Scenes of Hollywood Disaster Movies

introduction
Looking Back at Hollywood's Disaster Genre

Opening Remarks

At first glance it seems easy to grasp the genre of the disaster film. And while it's simple to rattle off names of disaster pictures like *The Towering Inferno, Airport, Twister* and *Titanic*, and even credit the likes of Irwin Allen, Ross Hunter, or even Alfred Hitchcock, as the creator of the disaster picture, understanding the development of the disaster film as a genre takes time and consideration.

While it's true that the memorable films and people like Hunter, Allen and Hitchcock played important roles in furthering the genre, even stabilizing it into a cohesive body, the disaster picture's origins go back to the early years of film itself. And while it had peaks and valleys, and general periods of stagnation, the genre grew stronger as the film industry progressed. In recent years the disaster movie has taken hold, becoming one of the most popular and profitable types of movies on theater screens today.

What makes a successful disaster movie, many might say, is an easy formula to follow – A good story, fantastic special effects, a first-rate cast, and talented direction are the obvious elements. But a lot can happen from formula to finished product, and even films which appear to have all the elements can falter, while those with little can reap box office rewards because of great marketing or a timely release.

"The bigger the tragedy, the bigger the audience," Producer Irwin Allen once quipped. "People chase fire engines, flock to car crashes. People thrive on tragedy. It's unfortunate, but in my case, it's fortunate."

Allen may have touched on the truth, but that truth expands way beyond the disaster picture and encompasses film as a whole. Audiences flock to dramas, horrors, science fiction flicks, thrillers, and even comedies, as an escape from reality. Whether they step into a theater to see a hockey-masked villain killing

13

teen-agers, or the sinking of an ocean liner, or spaceships visiting far-off planets, it's still the escape moviegoers are after.

The disaster film enables viewers to take part in a tragedy from the comfort of a movie theater, or their own living room couch. The experience of tragedy without real death, danger and destruction drives viewers to these films. The more real the experience, the more we as viewers want to experience it, to feel as if they really been there and survived. Even the theme park industry has caught on and in recent years, Universal Studios and Disney have brought the movie going experience to a new level, bringing movies off the big screen and introducing closer looks at disaster films like, *Earthquake, Jaws, Twister, Dante's Peak* and others.

Billions of dollars have been earned on the success of the disaster movie. *Titanic* alone pulled in more than $600 million making it the biggest moneymaking picture of all time. And that's just the tip of the iceberg. Disaster pictures over the decades have been some of the most financially successful pictures Hollywood has

produced.

And now, today's advances in technology are enabling moviemakers to bring the reality of the disaster film ever closer to the real thing. The computer-generated effects of *Twister* led to a new generation of disaster films as Hollywood realized the computer-generated simulations were so life-like that everything from tornados, to volcanic explosions, comet impacts, tidal waves and any imaginable disaster could be created with a series capable keystrokes. As the costs came in line new life was breathed into the disaster movie, and when *Twister* topped $200 million at the box office, Hollywood saw an opportunity and once again, just as in the 1970s, the genre flourished.

But with opportunity comes challenges, and with the challenges come the inevitable failures. Just as the genre swept through the 1970s with a string of successful pictures it burned out with a subsequent string of high-profile failures.

To uncover the full story behind the success, failure, past, present and future of the disaster film, one must look at the genre from many angles.

Chronologically, the genre has seen growth, but the disaster film of the 1920s was a mere experiment in filmmaking, while those of the 50s were more closely associated to the fears of the nation, and the true start of the genre in the 1970s stemmed from numerous factors like the advent of television, advances in special effects techniques, changes in the Hollywood system, among others.

Looking at the genre through those who helped give it life sheds light on the nature of filmmaking, the quest for box office success, fame, industry recognition and a host of other issues. Directors and producers like Irwin Allen, Ross Hunter, Alfred Hitchcock, Jennings Lang, Ronald Neame and others helped shape the genre through their films. Their struggles offer fascinating views from behind the scenes of some of Hollywood's most spectacular films.

The disasters themselves also offer an interesting view of the genre. Flood and water disasters like *The Poseidon Adventure* and *Titanic*; fire and explosion disasters like *The Towering Inferno, Dante's Peak, Volcano* and *When Time Ran Out*; collisions like *Meteor, Armageddon* and *Deep Impact*; attack disasters like *The Birds, Jaws, Bug* and *Swarm*; and the airline disasters of the *Airport* features each offer a glimpse at the progression of the genre and the quest for new and unusual directions to take the disaster picture.

Finally, the films themselves offer telling tales of history of Hollywood movie making. The stars, the directors, the production troubles, the successes and the failures offer probably the most interesting picture of the making of a great disaster.

The coming chapters will attempt to offer a full view of the history of the genre through its films and those who created them. Because, just as the horror film or the science fiction movies have had an unforgettable impact on the history of filmmaking, so has the disaster film. The rich and expansive tapestry of filmmaking is that much richer and that much more expansive because of the disasters on the silver screen.

one
I Feel a Disaster Coming On

Alfred Hitchcock promoting his 1963 classic, 'The Birds.'

Categorizing Disaster

O ften, the most logical method for finding one's way through a large collection — whether it be books, music or film — is to use logic and organization. That's why when paging through a film guide or walking through the average DVD or video store the organization is often by the type of film. The action/adventure pictures, the dramas, the classics, comedies and other categories help people focus their attention and direct them to where they wish to be. But rarely do we find a category for disaster pictures.

One might suspect it's because the genre is so small, or perhaps too specific, and that's a fair assessment. Therefore disaster pictures are dropped into other categories where they also fit. But while a film like *Armageddon* may fall under science fiction, *The Poseidon Adventure* will end up under adventure. And while *The Birds* will be categorized as horror, *Titanic* will be considered a drama. Others may end up under subjects like classics or suspense. And if you want to consider spoofs like *Airplane* and its sequel, as legitimate disaster films, the subject of comedy could be considered a home for at least two disaster pictures.

The disaster picture really came into its own as a genre in the early 1970s. Some would pinpoint the origin to the release of *Airport* in 1970. The success of the big-budget Universal feature led to a series of sequels that spanned the decade and, as mentioned earlier, spawned two spoofs of the series.

Aside from *Airport,* others credit producer Irwin Allen for the development of the disaster genre. Allen, who has long been referred to as the Master of Disaster, really took the disaster and turned it into an event. By casting major stars from past and current Hollywood, like Shelly Winters, Paul Newman, Fred Astaire, Faye Dunaway, Olivia DeHavilland, Henry Fonda, Michael Caine and others, and adding monstrous special

19

effects, Oscar-winning theme songs, and major promotional efforts, Allen turned the films into all-star spectacular events and often kept the audience wondering who would live and who would die.

But even if the 1970s was the era when the disaster genre took hold, the style of film actually took to the big screen years earlier. In fact, as far back as 1915 the elements that would make up a successful disaster picture were finding their way onto film. In the decades that followed countless films would touch upon the disaster to create emotion, suspense, thrills, horror and drama for viewers. Few of these films are actually categorized as true disaster pictures, but as mentioned, even "true disaster" films like the *Airport* series of films by Irwin Allen are not categorized as disaster pictures, because for many the category simply doesn't exist.

The Early Days

In the early days of the film industry, short films were the standard. When Thomas Edison's Kinetoscope offered the first films,

the coin-operated "peep viewers" presented a 20-second show. The shows were often of basic scenes, like a speeding train or a horse race. In time the features expanded, telling more of a story. The most successful film of these early years, *The Great Train Robbery,* can be viewed as the great-grandfather of the disaster picture, offering the action and suspense that would become standard elements of all disaster films to come. Other early mock-news footage, as far back as 1902 depicted erupting volcanoes.

In 1912, an Italian version of Lord Lytton's *The Last Days of Pompeii* again captured the disaster of an erupting volcano with 10,000 people fleeing its wrath.

When *Birth of a Nation* offered the first disastrous look at the Civil War in 1915, the film was a tremendous hit. D.W. Griffith's epic film touched on the vast tragedy of the war, but viewed it through its impact on two families that struggled through it, bringing the disaster down to a human level. Most disaster films of later years found this the easiest route for audience identification.

The King of Kings in 1927 by Cecile B DeMille was a biblical epic that captured a massive earthquake that hits during the Crucifixion, killing onlookers and helped expand the use of special effects to create awe on the big screen. Audiences were being drawn to the spectacular footage and Hollywood was quick to take note and expand on the concept.

The 1930s

In the 1930s the film disaster took a number of different forms, but most often catastrophic events in nature proved to be the ticket at the movies.

King Kong in 1933 brought a disaster in the size of a monstrous ape and the destruction came to modern day New York City. It still wasn't a textbook disaster picture, but Hollywood was getting closer and the carnage around the Empire State Building made for one of the most memorable disaster scenes in movie history.

The Last Days of Pompeii was remade by Hollywood in 1935 and again featured a climax with an erupting volcano creating fear for the crowds beneath it. It also created fear for the moviegoers who sat in the theater watching it. The film has been heralded for its use of special effects and the realism set the stage for more natural disasters that would find major success on the big screen.

San Francisco in 1936 captured the 1906 San Francisco earthquake. Directed by Woody Van Dyke with uncredited help from D.W. Griffith, the film used melodrama and a romantic plot with Clark Gable and Jeanette MacDonald to build to the climactic event that everyone was waiting for. Moviegoers were not disappointed by the destruction and the film was a hit.

Alfred Hitchcock's *Sabotage*, also in 1936, featured a bomb planted on a bus and the tragic explosion that follows. It was one of Hitchcock's first forays into disaster, and certainly not his last. *Lost Horizon* in 1937 again featured a plane crash while *Hurricane*, from director John Ford, was released that same year and climaxed with winds and the rains wreaking havoc on a small island.

Disaster up to this point was usually held

for the climactic scenes of a film that kept the films from actually evolving around the disasters themselves, as later films would do. The disaster was an element of the film, often what the film led up to.

In 1939, two major hit films utilized disasters to tell their stories. *Gone With The Wind* featured the disaster of the Civil War, as in *Birth of a Nation*, and again brought the war to a human level. But this time the sprawling scenery of a burned-out Atlanta and a struggle to survive created suspense, drama and characters the audience could love. *The Wizard of Oz* also brought disaster to a new level, because this time the trauma came at the beginning of the film, leading the way to the entire story that followed. While quite different from a standard disaster picture, the twister at the beginning was a spectacular visual effect for its time and set the stage for more trouble from Mother Nature on the big screen. *The Rains Came*, also in 1939, won an Oscar for its special effects and was another early natural disaster picture of note.

The 1940s

In 1940, Alfred Hitchcock returned to the disaster with *Foreign Correspondent* when a plane crash takes the film's major characters by surprise and created added suspense for moviegoers. Hitchcock began his 1943 film *Lifeboat* after the disaster had happened, leaving the characters to struggle for survival after their ship has been sunk during the war. The war provided the backdrop for these disasters and it is possibly because of the war that so few disaster pictures found life on the big screen. Moviegoers, during this period, looked for musicals and comedies to escape the trouble in reality.

The 1950s

The 1950s took disaster in several different directions. The first was a continuation of earlier films, but by now the disasters were becoming for central to the storyline, not just a major climax at the end.

Twentieth-Century Fox's *No Highway in the Sky* in 1951 was directed by Henry Koster and starred James Stewart as an aerodynamic engineer who theorizes that metal fatigue is a leading cause of plane crashes. Glynis Johns, Stewart's love interest in the film, and Marlene Dietrich, as a famous actress, are on a doomed flight that's the focus of Stewart's attention.

Titanic in 1953 chronicled the doomed ocean liner on its maiden voyage and used drama and character development to keep audiences watching and waiting for the inevitable iceberg. Barbara Stanwyck and Clifton Webb brought the story to life and the film earned an Academy Award for Best Story or Screenplay.

In 1954 it was back to disaster in the air when John Wayne starred in *The High and the Mighty* as a troubled pilot who takes over control of a crippled commercial plane flying over the Pacific Ocean. This time the film featured an all-star cast, including Claire Trevor, Laraine Day, Robert Stack and Jan Sterling. It was a Warner Bros. hit from Director William Wellman that used Cinemascope to thrill audiences. The film succeeded, taking in more than $6.1 million at the box office that year.

Then in 1956, Doris Day starred in *Julie,*

as the title character, an airline stewardess whose psychotic husband, played by Louis Jourdan, creates terror and suspense while the plane is in flight.

The second type of disaster picture that caused a stir throughout the 1950s was of the science fiction nature. As the cold war took hold the threat of danger in Hollywood came from monsters, often created by nuclear radiation and threatened the future of the entire planet. Some of the most memorable of this type of picture included *Them* (1954), *Godzilla* (1954), *It Came from Beneath the Sea* (1955), *The Beginning of the End* (1957), *The Blob* (1958) and *Earth vs. The Spider* (1958).

The third type of film that threatened worldwide disaster again came in the form of a science fiction picture, but this time, the threat came from outer space. Hollywood was playing its part as the United States and the world began exploring the unknown beyond earth. The fascination with other planets and what else was out there led to films like *War of the Worlds* (1952), *Invaders from Mars* (1953), *Invasion of* the Body Snatchers (1956) and *Invasion of the Saucer Men* (1957) as mutants threatening the future of mankind landed on our planet.

And in 1959, nuclear armageddon was the basis for a dramatic look at the demise of mankind when Anthony Perkins, Gregory Peck and Ava Gardner took to the big screen in *On the Beach*.

The 1960s

The 1960s seemed to put the threat from beyond the planet Earth away and began focusing the disasters from within. *The Devil at Four O'clock* in 1961 starred Spencer Tracy and Frank Sinatra on a fight against an erupting volcano on a small island in the South Pacific. *Atlantis, the Lost Continent*, also in 1961, featured Greek fishermen who discover the lost continent shortly before it blows up and *The Day the Earth Caught Fire* (1962) found the earth spinning out of control and headed straight for the sun all thanks to nuclear testing.

Alfred Hitchcock brought the disaster to a small town for *The Birds* in 1963. The suspense classic had flocks of birds attacking the small Northern California town of Bodega Bay and starred Tippi Hedren, Rod Taylor, Jessica Tandy and Suzanne Pleshette. The film was really one of the first full-fledged disaster pictures with feathered friends taking the part of the natural disaster as the stars struggled to survive. Hitchcock kept us wondering who would live and die and used special effects to make the terror look real. It was one of Hitchcock's biggest financial hits and most expensive pictures to make.

In 1964, *Failsafe* brought the threat of nuclear destruction back to the big screen as Henry Fonda, playing the president of the United States, sends a bomb to New York City, killing his own wife, so he can convince the Russians his first strike on the Soviet Union was an accident. The destruction was never shown, but the threat was all too real. *Seven Days in May*, also in 1964, brought an all-star cast including Burt Lancaster, Kirk Douglas, Ava Garner, Frederic March and others out with a look at the potential disaster behind a military coup in the United States and again the threat of nuclear destruction plays in the background.

Crack in the World in 1965 was another science fiction stab at disaster. This time underground nuclear testing causes a crack in the earth and a portion of the planet blasts off into outer space. The film was a throwback to the late 1950s and was about the last of its type.

The remainder of the decade steered away from disaster pictures. Perhaps it was because the war in Vietnam came crashing into American living rooms through the nightly news. Assassinations of our leaders also became all too common and racial tensions had erupted in city streets bringing disaster closer to home. Disaster was no longer an escape, but a very real part of our everyday lives.

In 1970, however, the disaster picture took a grand step forward and came back in a big way.

two
Disaster in the Air

A Decade for Disaster

In 1970 the disaster picture jumped to a whole new level and caught Hollywood and moviegoers by surprise. But once the disaster genre came to life it seemed as if there was no stopping it, and through the course of the decade the disaster picture would become one of the most successful types of film of its era.

Disaster films certainly became some of the biggest moneymakers of the decade. The success of the genre would result in remakes of some previous classics like *King Kong* and *Hurricane*, and spawned spoofs like *Airplane* in addition to the string of features with harrowing dramas in the air, at sea, on land, and in space. The 1970s hits brought in more than $230 million, far surpassing the production of the pictures, which usually cost less than $10 million a piece to make. However, as the decade wore on the disasters became more costly and the hits became fewer and farther between. But in 1970, the sky was the limit.

Universal

By 1970, Universal had come a long way. Founded as Universal City by nickelodeon owner Carl Laemmle, Universal Studios opened in Hollywood in 1915 and was mostly known for small, undistinguished pictures. That was until the 1930s when its bread and butter came from a series of successful horror films, including *Dracula, Frankenstein, The Mummy, The Wolf Man* and countless others. Through the 1940s, 50s and 60s, the studio expanded its reach, exploring a variety of genres and even churning out several big pictures each year in addition to its string of lower-budget features.

In the early 1960s MCA, the talent agency headed by Lew Wasserman, took over Universal and moved into the world of filmmaking. MCA clients like Jimmy Stewart and Alfred Hitchcock came along and the studio profited through most of the decade.

When Alfred Hitchcock took up residence on the studio lot, he offered the studio one of the earliest full-fledged disaster pictures — *The Birds*. Although often categorized as a horror, Hitchcock's films rarely offered the gore of the standard horror film. *The Birds* used stars; special effects, drama and suspense to tell its story, and helped develop the format the many later disaster pictures would follow. However, *The Birds* offered an anti-climactic finale, unlike most standard disaster pictures. But Universal was happy with the hit and continued its relationship with Hitchcock, although the director never tackled a film like it again.

In 1969 all the major studios, including Universal, were hit with a bad year. Although most of the studios were succeeding with television ventures, the big screen was facing tough competition from the relatively young medium of TV. Studios spent more to make "big" movies. Major stars, exotic locations, fabulous effects were being used to create something more spectacular onscreen than on

television. However, the public wasn't buying and Hollywood found itself hit with some major losses. Twentieth Century Fox lost $27.5 million that year, while MGM lost $35.4 million. Universal, Paramount and Warner Bros. and other major studios also suffered, but because Universal's television efforts were so solid, the losses were not as great.

The losses continued through 1971 and it has been reported that jointly the studios lost more than $500 million during these troubled years. It would take most of the studios several years to fully recover, but not Universal. In 1970 it came up a winner when it released *Airport*, which, in many ways, jump-started the disaster genre that would swell throughout the decade.

Airport

In January 1967 a major snowstorm whipped through the Midwest, hammering Chicago with some of the worst weather it had seen in years. O'Hare International Airport was shut down for three days, affecting the more than 35 million travelers the airport was designed to serve, leaving thousands stranded with no place to go and no way to get there.

The storm inspired writer Arthur Hailey to write a book about the trouble and the dangers facing a major metropolitan airport like O'Hare during a terrible blizzard. The result was *Airport*.

The book became a bestseller, spending 65 weeks at number one on the bestseller list, and furthered the career of Hailey as a world-renowned author. Hailey had already found success in bookstores and on movie screens after his earlier novel, *Hotel*, became a bestseller and was made into a lavish screen hit in 1967. *Airport* solidified his reputation and led to a number of other book-to-film opportunities.

Hotel, in many ways, is another precursor to the disaster picture. The similarities between it and *Airport* in structure and style are quite obvious. A glamorous setting, all-star cast, drama, suspense, a dash of humor and a lavish production were all part of the style of the disaster film and would be for years to come. But the production and style of the films cannot

simply be credited to Hailey. Actually, it was producer Ross Hunter who had created the style many years earlier. And it is Hunter, who earns much of the credit for launching the all-star disaster picture.

Born Martin Fuss, Ross Hunter was a schoolteacher in Cleveland until World War II when he went to war, serving in the U.S. Army. After the war he briefly returned to teaching, but found his interest in Hollywood was too great and obtained a screen test at Paramount Pictures. Eventually he caught the attention of a Columbia Pictures talent scout and earned a long-term studio contract as an actor. His name was changed to Ross Hunter.

Hunter never amounted to much as an actor and eventually returned to teaching, this time at a dramatic school. He also began producing shows for the San Fernando Valley Theater, using Hollywood friends like Virginia Grey and Lucille Ball as his stars. Once again he caught the notice of Hollywood and Universal executive Leonard Goldstein offered Hunter a two-week assignment to cut the production costs of a film called *Flame of Araby* in 1952. Hunter found a way to streamline camera operations and saved the production $172,000. His success led to other production cutting jobs at Universal as a full-time employee earning $75 a week. By 1953 he had moved up to associate producer, earning $200 a week. When his film *Take Me to Town* became a hit that year, Hunter convinced the studio to let him make a series of glamorous women's pictures.

What followed was a long list of hit films with glamorous leading ladies in lavish settings facing drama and suspense. His stars were often obtained at limited salaries, but were dressed by leading designers in gowns and jewels. The films became known as soap operas and were often remakes of earlier pictures. Some of his most memorable films include *All I Desire* with Barbara Stanwyck, *Magnificent Obsession* with Jane Wyman, *Imitation of Life, Portrait in Black* and *Madame X* with Lana Turner, *Backstreet* with Susan Hayward, and *Midnight Lace* with Doris Day.

In 1961, he established Ross Hunter Productions and signed a long-term deal with Universal, earning him millions and forming a partnership that would last through the 1960s.

By 1969, Hunter's tenure at Universal was coming to an end, as he would leave the studio in 1971, but before he did, he offered Universal his glamorous version of Arthur Hailey's *Airport* and the film would become the studio's biggest hit.

Hunter assembled and all-star cast of current and old Hollywood. Burt Lancaster, Dean Martin, Jacqueline Bisset, Helen Hayes, Jean Seberg, Dana Wynter, Barbara Hale, Lloyd Nolan, Maureen Stapleton, Van Heflin, Jessie Royce Landis, Barry Nelson and George Kennedy took on the major roles. Behind the scenes, Hunter obtained Director George Seaton, whose memorable efforts included *The Country Girl, Miracle on 34th Street* and *Teacher's Pet* to direct the picture, and to make the cast look its best, Edith Head, who moved to Universal in 1968, after 30 years at Paramount, oversaw the costumes for the lavish production. Filming took about 15 weeks.

The total budget, about $10 million, was still quite expensive for its day, but Hunter's proven track record enabled the studio to take the risk.

The film has been called *Grand Hotel* on wings and revolves around an airport and a Boeing 707. Several different storylines are intertwined to bring the characters together on a fateful flight. Burt Lancaster portrays a workaholic airport manager whose marriage to Dana Wynter is crumbling while he's slowly falling in love with Jean Seberg, an airline PR director. George Kennedy, an airline maintenance man is called into work after a plane to get stuck in snow at the end of the runway.

Because the runway is shut down the airport is forced to use a secondary runway that flies over a residential neighborhood, angering the folks who live there. Protesters bring picket signs and threats of firing Lancaster lead to the inevitable shutdown of the airport. But before that can happen, a desperate bomb-carrying man, played by Van Heflin, tries to blow up the 707

he's aboard and the plane is forced to return to the airport before it crashes. Piloted by Dean Martin, who's having an affair with pregnant stewardess Jacqueline Bisset, a large hole in the side of the plane from the explosion puts the passengers and crew in jeopardy. Bisset is injured in the explosion after the crew, with help from stowaway Helen Hayes, tries to get the bomb away from Heflin.

In order to land the plane needs the longest runway available, which happens to be the one with the stuck plane on it, therefore, the ground crew must work feverishly to get the plane stuck in the snow free and open the runway in time for Martin to land his plane safely.

Filmed in Technicolor and in Todd-AO, for a brilliant, larger-than-life look, the feature was released in February, 1970 and heralded as "a handsome, often dramatically involving epitaph to a bygone brand of filmmaking," according to *Variety*.

The New York Times was not as kind, calling it "an immensely silly film," but went on to add, "It will probably entertain millions of people who no longer care very much about movies."

The reviewer was right about one thing; the film certainly entertained a lot of viewers. In its initial release that year, *Airport* took in $45.3 million, becoming Universal's biggest hit to date. And when Oscar time rolled around the following year the film earned 10 nominations. Helen Hayes was the only winner, though, coming away with a Best Supporting Actress award for her performance.

The success of airport can be credited to various factors. The suspense and adventure of a crippled airliner filled with passengers was a fairly new experience for Hollywood. Airline travel was finally becoming a more common form of travel the mass public was experiencing, so many could relate to the situation. And there was, and still is, a certain amount of fear associated with airline travel, but in addition, there was a certain prestige or glamour tied to it as well. The first-rate cast of well-known actors provided identifiable characters the audience could relate to, as well. This, in effect, enabled the all-star pictures to steer away from character development and concentrate more on story and special effects; yet, because the faces were familiar we were already attached to the actors themselves, so the audience was emotionally involved. This would become a staple for the most successful of disaster pictures.

Another factor for the box office interest was that special effects, using miniatures and matte paintings had advanced a great deal and the studios could achieve greater heights in making the danger look real.

Airport was a true "event" picture. Its Technicolor look and widescreen format with major stars offered something viewers couldn't find on television and once the movie got off to a roaring start, word of mouth enabled the success to continue. It was the second highest-grossing picture of the year, behind Paramount's *Love Story*, which earned $50 million. *MASH*, another hit that year, was *Airport*'s closest competition for box-office draw, but it fell well behind, placing third for 1970 earning only $30 million.

three
Disaster on the High Seas

The Master of Disaster

It was 1968 when writer Paul Gallico penned "The Poseidon Adventure," a harrowing tale surrounding a band of passengers aboard an ocean liner that capsizes after being hit by a massive tidal wave. Gallico reportedly came across the idea for the story many years earlier during a stormy voyage on The Queen Mary. And The Queen Mary herself came close to capsizing during a storm in 1936 when passengers later told reporters they felt the ship might capsize.

The book caught the attention of producer Irwin Allen, who thought the story would make a top-notch feature film. Allen claimed he read the galley proofs of the book in 24-hours and later bought the film rights. The film would be something of a departure as well as a return for Allen.

Allen's Path to the Poseidon

Irwin Allen came to Hollywood in 1938 after working in journalism and advertising in New York with a variety of jobs. He held positions like radio news commentator, magazine editor, syndicated newspaper columnist, and literary agent before hearing the call of Hollywood. Allen's early work in the entertainment business came as a quiz show host in the early days of television, but he turned to filmmaking in 1948, acting as co-producer of *It's Only Money*, an RKO production starring Frank Sinatra, Jane Russell and Groucho Marx. The feature wasn't released until 1951, when it was retitled *Double Dynamite*, but gave Allen his first taste of movie making. In 1953, he directed a documentary entitled *The Sea Around Us*, which was based on the book of the same name by Rachel Carson. The film was a study of the fauna, flora and fish that populate the ocean and earned Allen an Academy Award that year for Best Documentary.

The success of the documentary led Allen

to follow up the work with another film four years later based on another non-fiction work, *The Story of Mankind,* in addition to steady work on other features like *The Animal World* in 1956 and *The Big Circus* in 1959. Following this period Allen transitioned into science fiction adventure tales, filming *The Lost World* in 1960, *Voyage to the Bottom of the Sea* in 1961 and *Five Weeks in a Balloon* in 1962.

For Allen the 1960s offered him his greatest success through a string of hit television shows, mostly venturing again into the world of science fiction. *Lost in Space, Land of the Giants, The Time Tunnel,* and another ocean adventure, *Voyage to the Bottom of the Sea,* brought the producer fame and fortune. But while his success came in television, he longed for success on the big screen.

Teaming with Fox for Disaster at Sea

Allen brought Gallico's capsized ocean liner adventure to the attention of Twentieth Century Fox, which was reportedly hesitant about bankrolling the expensive picture. Fox had recently pulled itself out of a difficult decade after a close call with bankruptcy in the 1960s. *Cleopatra*, starring Elizabeth Taylor and Richard Burton, brought the studio to the brink of bankruptcy during the early 1960s when delays and rising production costs hit the studio with a bill for an estimated $40 million dollars to produce and market the film. While the film pulled in millions less than its cost after its release in 1963, the studio struggled to make ends meet.

Fox's film productions dwindled; executives sold off back lots and nearly anything that wasn't nailed down to stay afloat. Finally, in 1965, after five dark years, Fox came back with a hit in *The Sound of Music*, but it would be several more years, mixed with successes and failures, before the studio found itself on more solid ground. By the early 1970s the studio was back in action, and after seeing the success of Universal's *Airport*, Fox probably felt a capsized ocean liner might make for good box office. Allen got an ok and soon was in business.

But even though he had the go ahead of

the studio, bankrolling the picture would prove more difficult than he planned. The expensive budget caused delays in the start of the picture twice and it wasn't until Allen lured outside investors to match Fox's investment in the film that the producer obtained the funds to make the picture he envisioned.

Like *Airport,* casting would again be crucial to the success of the picture. An all-star cast of recognizable faces and names would offer credibility and class to the feature and a cast of up-and-coming actors, along with old-time Hollywood would help the film draw fans from several demographics.

A Cast of Stars

Gene Hackman was hired as the star, portraying Reverend Frank Scott, a preacher who helps lead a group of passengers to safety through the ship turned upside-down. Hackman's earlier starring credits included *Marooned* in 1969 and *Bonnie and Clyde* in 1967. Hackman would also win an Oscar for his performance in *The French Connection* in 1971 and would follow the role with Allen's feature.

Ernest Borgnine, who earned an Academy Award for his leading role in *Marty* in 1955, had a long career in Hollywood and was signed to the role of Mike Rogo, a cop on the cruise with his wife. Stella Stevens, who starred in numerous films in the 1960s like *Girls, Girls, Girls* with Elvis Presley and *The Nutty Professor* with Jerry Lewis, signed on as Borgnine's wife, a former prostitute, Linda Rogo. And another Oscar-winner, Shelly Winters, who had a long career in Hollywood with films like *The Diary of Anne Frank* and *A Place in the Sun,* took the role of Belle Rosen.

Other noteworthy actors from old Hollywood included Jack Albertson, Red Buttons, Roddy McDowall and Leslie Nielsen. In addition, Carol Lynley, Pamela Sue Martin and Eric Shea rounded out the band of survivors.

The story erupts at midnight on New Year's Eve when the passenger liner, the S.S. Poseidon, is struck by a 90-foot tidal wave which is the result of an earthquake beneath the sea.

The ship capsizes in a dramatic sequence that has the entire cast tossing around as the ship turns over in the water.

Reverend Frank Scott, played by Hackman, is a rebellious preacher who often goes against the rules of the church. He tries to encourage the surviving passengers to climb for their lives, but only nine survivors take him up on his offer to lead them to safety — an elderly couple, Manny and Belle Rosen, who are on their way to Greece; a New York detective, Mike Rogo and his wife Linda on their second honeymoon; a young brother and sister, Robin and Susan Shelby sailing to meet their parents; a haberdasher named James Martin; a pop singer named Nonnie Parry, whose band was traveling to a concert and offered free music in exchange for passage; and Acres, a ship's waiter.

The survivors climb a metal Christmas tree to escape the soon-to-be flooding grand ballroom and travel through, steam, fire and the flooding upside-down ship trying to find the propeller shaft at the bottom, which is now the top and happens to be the thinnest part of the hull

and the most likely place for rescuers to come through. Along the way several of the survivors are killed leaving the remaining passengers to struggle on.

Making of a Disaster

Allen hired Ronald Neame as director. Neame had a long career in Hollywood as a cinematographer and director, dating back to the 1930s. Some of his most memorable directorial efforts included *The Chalk Garden, Gambit*, and *The Prime of Miss Jean Brodie*, among others.

For filming, Allen and Neame went the unusual route of shooting the picture in chronological order. While not the norm because it often costs more to make a movie using this method, for *The Poseidon Adventure* it proved workable for several reasons. First, because the actors were mainly confined to one set with the stars all filming much of the feature together, and second, because the characters became more dirty, bruised and tired as their climb through the ship progressed, it worked to have the actors film the feature that way as well so their costumes and appearance would deteriorate as filming carried on.

Early footage of the ship upright was filmed aboard The Queen Mary, Gallico's inspiration for the book, which was berthed in Long Beach, California. Sets of the ship upside down were constructed using blueprints and photographs of the real ocean liner, including the boiler room, where the major climax of the picture takes place. A miniature 23-foot replica of the ship was also constructed for the exterior shots when the ship is actually capsized by the massive wave.

The actors were asked to do much of the stunt work themselves, except for some of the riskier efforts. Shelly Winters was called upon to gain as much as 35 pounds for her role as an elderly Jewish woman, a task she would later regret because she would never be able to lose the weight. Production took 14 weeks, with 11 weeks of filming the capsized portion of the feature. The cast spent most of the time immersed in water or surrounded by fire, explosions and steam and many recalled it as a difficult project.

A Hit Disaster

The film opened on December 12, 1972 and instantly found an audience. Moviegoers were thrilled by the action, suspense and effects, as well as the all-star cast. Allen took the disaster picture to a new level and expanded on the danger and suspense of *Airport*. *The Poseidon Adventure*, at a final cost of $10 million, was the second highest grossing picture of 1972, taking in $42 million at the U.S. box office that year. *The Godfather* was the top box office winner in 1972.

Critics were not as kind to the picture and many of the actors were wasted, according to some reviews, because of a weak screenplay by Stirling Silliphant. The direction from Neame and production by Allen were singled out as highlights of the film, as well as the astounding visual effects which drew most moviegoers to the big screen.

With 1973 came the awards for the successful feature. An Academy Award for Best Music went to the hit song "The Morning After" from the film and the feature also earned

a Special Achievement Oscar for its visual
effects. Academy Award nominations for the
film went to Shelly Winters as Best Supporting
Actress, and to the feature for art direction,
cinematography, costume design, film editing,
musical score and sound. The hit song was
also nominated for a Golden Globe and Shelly
Winters took home a Golden Globe for her
supporting role.

Allen had finally landed on the scene as
a major motion picture producer and soon Fox
was already waiting for a follow-up disaster
to recapture the success of *The Poseidon
Adventure*. Allen was only too happy to oblige.

four
Burning Down the House

Irwin Allen Strikes Twice

Most often, the disaster picture of the 1970s was rooted in man's greed and the ramifications of that greed. Usually in an attempt to profit, cut costs, or beat the clock, man underestimates Mother Nature and disaster comes calling. While not so much the case with *Airport,* the theme became embedded in the genre after *The Poseidon Adventure*'s success in 1972. The ship's owner, against advice from Captain Leslie Nielsen, orders the ship to go at full speed, putting it on a collision course with the massive tidal wave that capsizes the ship. Other features like *Jaws, Earthquake, Avalanche* and *Meteor* also chose that route, having man avoid or ignore the danger, only to have it come at a high price.

Possibly the quintessential disaster picture using all the themes and elements including expansive special effects, an all-star cast and a payback for man's ignorance and greed was *The Towering Inferno*, which helped the disaster picture peak in 1975. In addition to the *Towering Inferno, Airport 75* and *Earthquake* made 1975 a banner year for disasters.

Producer Irwin Allen would go onto produce and direct numerous disaster films following the success of *The Towering Inferno,* but never would his vision be as realized as it was on this picture. The financial rewards of the film helped dry the ink of the disaster formula that led to many of the pictures that followed. For Allen it proved that *The Poseidon Adventure* would not make him a one-hit wonder and it was after the release of *The Towering Inferno* that Irwin earned himself the title of Master of Disaster.

Another Disaster for Allen

Following the box-office success of *The Poseidon Adventure* in December 1972 and honors at the Academy Awards in early 1973, producer Irwin Allen began thinking of a follow-up to the feature. Twentieth Century Fox easily gave Allen the go-ahead for another film and increased his budget from $10 million for *The Poseidon Adventure* to nearly $15 million for his next effort. All Allen needed was an appropriate project. With the sea taken care and the *Airport* series covering the skies, disaster on land probably seemed the next locale to attack.

Sometime in mid-1973 Allen came across a copy of a book entitled "The Glass Inferno," by Thomas N. Scortia and Frank M. Robinson, which tells the story of a deadly fire in a skyscraper. With Fox in search of a disaster follow-up the studio purchased the film rights for some $400,000 and Allen began preparing for his movie. But before pre-production began Allen learned that eight weeks earlier Warner Bros. had purchased the rights to another burning skyscraper novel called "The Tower," by Richard Martin Stern for about $390,000 with the intention of making its own disaster picture. The similarities between the two books were striking and Allen proposed that instead of creating competing features, Warner Bros. and Fox join forces and use both books to create one magnificent disaster picture.

For the collaboration the studios agreed to split the cost down the middle with Fox reaping the rewards of the lucrative domestic box office and Warners taking the rest of the world. Once the deal was inked, the screenplay was completed and casting began. In March 1974, an all-star cast was announced that included some of the leading action and drama stars of the day, along with some of Hollywood's legends of yesteryear. Paul Newman as the architect who designs the building and Steve McQueen as the fire chief shared the lead, with Faye Dunaway, Richard Chamberlin, Robert Wagner and Susan Blakely rounding out the other major roles in the cast. William Holden, Fred Astaire and Jennfier Jones captured Hollywood's golden era, while Robert Vaughan, O.J. Simpson, Jack Collins, and Allen's wife, Sheila Matthews, rounded out the cast. In addition, Susan Flannery, who got her star in Allen's TV series *Voyage to the Bottom of the Sea* and had recently earned an Emmy Award for her work on the soap opera *Days of Our*

Lives was cast in the film and Mike Lookinland, best known for his role of Bobby Brady on *The Brady Bunch*, portrayed one of two youngsters rescued in the blaze by Paul Newman.

Many of the key figures behind the making of *The Poseidon Adventure* were drawn into Allen's new picture. Screenwriter Sterling Silliphant helped create the script combining both books on which the story is based and the title combined the titles of both books as well. Silliphant incorporated the seven major characters from each book, but the major challenge was in handling the climax of the film. While "The Glass Tower" features exploding water tanks that douse the fire, "The Tower" relied on a harrowing life-line rescue by moving guests from the burning building to an adjacent building. Silliphant decided to use both endings and double the danger and special effects.

Other *Poseidon* staff included production designer William Creber and costume designer Paul Zastupnevich who brought reality to the sets and costumes, Harold Kress who was brought in again as film editor, Sidney Marshall, who was again the associate producer, and Tom Cranham, who had worked with Allen in his TV work as well as feature films, came on board as a special effects illustrator. For direction, Allen hired John Guillerman, who directed *Skyjacked* in 1972, to direct most of the picture, but Allen himself chose to direct the major action sequences. And a number of the extras that portrayed passengers on the ill-fated *Poseidon*, this time found themselves inside Allen's burning high-rise.

The Making of a Disaster

Irwin Allen originally planned for star Steve McQueen to portray the skyscraper's architect, with Newman taking the role of the fire chief, however McQueen opted for a casting change, preferring he play the fire chief and Allen agreed. Since both McQueen and Newman were the lead actors, Allen took steps to make the two stars happy. At McQueen's insistence both he and Newman were given the exact number of lines of dialogue in the script and both were paid $1 million in salary with a

7.5 percent cut of the box office receipts. And both men were credited as stars of the picture with staggered billing in the posters and ads for the film, as well as the opening and closing credits.

To prepare for his role as fire chief, Steve McQueen had meetings with two fire chiefs in the Los Angeles area who were brought in as technical advisers for the film. During one meeting, McQueen got first-hand experience when Goldwyn Studios caught fire and both chiefs headed to the scene. McQueen tagged along and at one point donned protective gear and a fire helmet and assisted the fire fighters with the blaze. One firefighter apparently noticed the star, saying "Steve McQueen! My wife will never believe this!" McQueen replied, "Neither will mine." McQueen was married to actress Ali MacGraw.

On the set, McQueen refused to give interviews and both he and Faye Dunaway asked that they not be approached by the many who visited the set during production.

Dunaway recalled that the major cast, as well as the producers and director were all part of a package deal worked out by a team of major Hollywood agents. Dunaway said the deal gave the agents 10 percent of the entire budget for the film, which left the stars with little representation on the working conditions or their part in the project. "I remembered then that I had fought with the agents about taking this part in the first place," Dunaway wrote in her autobiography. "But they had argued it would be good for my career, and there was the fact that Paul and Steve were both going to be in it. But at the end of the day, it was the star machine at it again, grinding up anyone who got in the way."

The actress also explained that Allen had a vision for the film and exerted his strength throughout the production and found that even though Guillerman was the director of the filming of the actors that "you could feel the hot breath of Irwin on his neck at all times."

Filming began around May, 1974 and continued into August with four camera crews working simultaneously with the actors scenes, the actions sequences and the special effects shots that were required. Matte paintings of the large skyscraper were combined with actual footage of the San Francisco skyline for some scenes that placed the fake building in the city and location shooting in San Francisco captured the entrance to the building, which was actually the Bank of America building. And interior shots of the scenic elevators were filmed at the Hyatt Regency Hotel in downtown San Francisco as well, while the exterior of Richard Chamberlin and Susan Blakely's home was another San Francisco locale on Vallejo Street.

For other footage of the burning building a miniature, which was approximately 100-feet tall was constructed to burn on cue. In addition, 57 sets on eight Fox soundstages were used in the making of the film. All but eight of the sets were destroyed in the making and four complete camera crews were required to capture the production. And with countless extras and some 300 stunt people, *The Towering Inferno* became the biggest production ever at the Fox studios.

The Harrowing Tale

The film begins with the completion of the largest building in San Francisco, a 138-story glass tower that dominates the city's skyline. Dedication ceremonies featured leaders from entertainment, politics and business who are invited to the cutting of the ribbon and a lavish party atop the skyscraper, which houses both business and residential occupants.

A small fire on the 81st floor breaks out in a storage room and cutbacks in wiring are blamed. Soon the fire ignites insulation, shelves of paint and other solvents and the fire begins to grow, expanding to other floors. As the fire spreads the fire department is called in, but because the fire is so high it proves impossible to fight and the fire chief orders the guests to evacuate the building. However, the elevators are unusable after a group of guests crowd onto one that opens on the floor with the fire and they are killed. One stairway is blocked by cement and another one, filled with smoke, is hit with a gas explosion, trapping the guests on the upper floors.

The only exit is a scenic elevator that travels down the side of the building, but it too is knocked from commission by the fire and the only means of escape is by attaching a cable to the building next door and moving people across one by one. But as time runs out and the fire grows closer a last-ditch effort to put out the fire is made when water tanks atop the building are blown up and a torrent of raging water pours down, putting out the fire and taking a few more celebrity lives in the process.

Released on December 14, 1974, the film brought in an estimated $57 million for Fox in its domestic release and some $116 million worldwide, giving Warners an estimated $59 million take. The final budget totaled out at $14,733,000, costing each studio less than $7.5 million to produce.

The film was the event movie of the year, but again critics were mixed with many calling it a spectacular adventure, but some criticizing its poor use of talent and mediocre storytelling. Pauline Kael of *The New Yorker* wrote, "Despite the gruesome goings on inside the world's tallest funeral pyre, a few performers manage to be minimally attractive. Paul Newman had the

sense to look embarrassed, which, in addition to him looking remarkably pretty and fit, helps things along."

Rex Reed of the *New York Daily News* wrote that "Newman and McQueen could make me believe anything. The sheer force of their opposing presence ignites and gives the film an aura of excitement it might otherwise not had without them."

All in all, the film was a resounding success and was named one of the more memorable pictures of the year and third biggest moneymaker of 1975, behind *Jaws* and *One Flew Over the Cuckoo's Nest*.

When Oscar time came around in early 1975 the film earned several important nominations. Irwin Allen earned his first Best Picture nomination, while John Williams found his score nominated for Best Music, Original Dramatic Score, and Herman Lewis and Theodore Soderberg were nominated for Best Sound. In addition, Fred Astaire earned a nomination as Best Supporting Actor. In the end, however, the only awards the film walked off with were for Best Cinematography, Best Film Editing, and Best Song.

The feature also earned several Golden Globe Awards, including Astaire for Best Supporting Actor and Susan Flannery for Most Promising Newcomer. Other nominations that didn't earn awards went to Jennifer Jones for her supporting role, Sterling Silliphant for his screenplay and Best Original Score for the song "We May Never Love Like This Again."

Allen was now well on his way with two major hits behind him and looked forward to hanging onto his title as Master of Disaster. He had several other notable projects to offer up for public scrutiny, however, nothing would ever equal the success of his first two disaster features.

five
I Feel the Earth Move

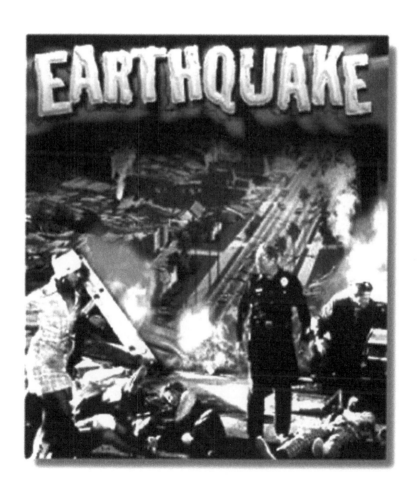

Disaster Landscape Expands

Jennings Lang had been around Hollywood a long time. And much like Irwin Allen, his career took him in various directions before landing soundly in the world of disaster films.

He went to Hollywood in 1938 as a practicing attorney opening an office as an agent. In 1940 he left his private practice to join the offices of the Jaffe Agency and within two years he was made a partner and vice president. He later served as president of the agency. By 1950 Lang was considered one of Hollywood's top agents when he left Jaffe to join MCA's agency. And in 1952 he became vice president MCA's television division and got involved in all aspects of operations and took a place on the board of directors. He eventually took charge of program development and was the force behind shows like *Wagon Train, Bachelor Father* and *McHale's Navy*. Lang eventually helped launched MCA Universal's telefilms; full-length features made for TV. This directed him toward theatrical motion pictures. Jennings Lang Presentations released full-length motion pictures like *Play Misty For Me* and *High Plains Drifter* in the early 70s. In 1975 he took over the *Airport* series of films, launching *Airport '75*, and found success with another major disaster picture and a revolutionary new film process. The film was *Earthquake* and the process was Sensurround.

Lang's success came from the fact that his background in television enabled him to produce films under a limited budget, most often using television crews and actors to keep costs low. When his films succeeded at the box office the studio made millions and enabled Lang to head back into production with another feature. Even though, like Irwin Allen, his films were often panned by critics, their success with the audience was all that mattered and he found himself promising to give the public what it wanted — until the public decided it didn't want it anymore.

Lang had acquired the talents of Charlton Heston for *Airport '75* and Universal, the studio producing the film, sent Heston the script for *Earthquake* in December 1973. After negotiating his salary and requiring a rewrite of the script to further develop his character, Heston agreed to do the film, which began pre-production in January 1974.

Once Heston was signed to the lead, and Mark Robson was hired to direct the picture, the rest of the casting took place with Ava Gardner cast as Heston's troubled wife and Genevieve Bujold cast as the other woman in the trio's love triangle. Heston never felt strongly about Gardner in the role of his wife and later admitted he wished he "performed more professionally in the scenes with her." He was, however, fond of Bujold and did better in his scenes with her. In the end, though, Heston claimed that while *Earthquake* was one of his most successful films, it was also one of those he was most disappointed over his performance in.

Universal's *Earthquake* was one of Hollywood's biggest productions in 1974 with vast special effects, hundreds of extras in massive scenes. Others in the cast included Lorne Greene who was ironically cast as Ava Gardner's father, when in fact he and Gardner were roughly the same age. George Kennedy, Victoria Principal, Richard Roundtree, Marjoe Gortner, Barry Sullivan, Lloyd Nolan, Walter Mathau and Monica Lewis rounded out the cast. George Fox and Mario Puzo received writing credit for the script.

Sounds Like a Disaster

To offer the full effects of the disaster, Lang helped developed a sound process that would enable viewers to feel the rumbling and vibrations from the quakes and destruction on the big screen. Prior to *Earthquake*, movie soundtracks were unable to process sound at very low frequencies, but with Lang's innovation, a special generator was used at certain points in the film to trigger several large subwoofer speakers which provided the low sounds of the rumbling quakes. Christened as Sensurround, the process was used to promote the film, offering a unique film going experience. The process was so successful that it was used in three more films and is considered a forerunner to the digital sound experience used in theaters today.

While not as successful as *The Towering Inferno*, *Earthquake* earned roughly $36 million at the box office after its release in November 1974, making it one of the successes of the year. And like most disaster pictures, the film earned mediocre reviews from the critics while fans turned out to see the special effects and the stars in danger. The special effects were applauded by many and even earned an award for Special Achievement for visual effects at the Academy Awards that year. The film also earned an Oscar for Best Sound and was nominated for Best Art Direction-Set Decoration. And the film was nominated for a Golden Globe for Best Dramatic Motion Pictures and John Williams earned a Golden Globe nomination for Best Original Score.

Another Lang Production

In addition to *Earthquake* and the *Airport* series, Lang also launched another quasi-disaster picture that found limited success. *Rollercoaster* in 1977 took the genre in a new direction when it headed to the amusement park for suspense and disaster.

In the film Timothy Bottoms portrays an extortionist who is sabotaging rollercoaster tracks and demands a million dollars in order to stop his destruction. Using actual footage from some of the country's best-known amusement parks the film succeeded more as a suspense film with George Segal as a safety inspector trying to stop the destruction. Others in the cast included Richard Widmark, Paula Prentiss and Henry Fonda. Directed by James Goldstone, the feature received mixed reviews with some praising the film as a cat and mouse type thriller while others called it feeble. The feature was also released in Sensurround, but did not find the success of its predecessor. But Jennings Lang saw life in the *Airport* series and continued his efforts in that direction.

six
Exposing the Horror of Disaster

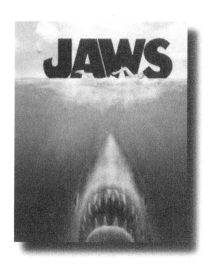

Mixing Disaster & Horror

Following the success of *Airport, The Poseidon Adventure, The Towering Inferno* and *Earthquake* Hollywood began finding a host of other projects that used the disaster as a major plot device. Soon a lengthy list of copies would be churned out, and by 1975 the genre had reached its peak with its greatest successes, but several noteworthy films in 1975 took the disaster picture in new directions.

Horror was a well established genre in Hollywood, and the concept of mixing it with disaster was not necessarily a new one, but the growth and success of the disaster picture helped horror filmmakers explore new avenues of horror. Mainly the standard horror picture had been a battle of good against evil. Most often villains like vampires, monsters and madmen were on the loose and had to be stopped. In the

1950s horror sometimes found itself merging with science fiction and films like *Invasion of the Body Snatchers* or *Them* offered disaster on a larger scale, but the it was usually a monster that represented the evil to be conquered. In the 1970s, with the success of the disaster picture, horror tried to take the ordinary or normal aspects of our world and create fear. Much like Alfred Hitchcock did in 1963 with *The Birds*, films now wanted disaster closer to home and something much more easy to come by. This type of horror didn't simply place good against evil or progress with a body count, but unfolded with a different form of natural disaster and offer its impact on a group of people. Two films in 1975 illustrate this mutation of the disaster film. One came from a young Hollywood director at the start of a brilliant career. The other feature was from a director at the end of his long career in Hollywood.

A Horror with Teeth

Steven Spielberg made a name for himself as one of the most successful and prolific directors in Hollywood. His rise to fame started in television and some noteworthy television shows and TV movies led to the big screen. He's since broken box office records with hits like *Jurassic Park* and earned Academy Awards for *Schindler's List* and *Saving Private Ryan*. But it was a long road, paved with successes, a few failures and a lot of hard work.

The Sugarland Express became the director's first major Hollywood feature film. And although the film has earned some critical acclaim over the years, it was a box office failure when it was released in 1974. It was disappointing for the director that the film didn't succeed, but by the time of its release Spielberg was already hard at work on a new film called *Jaws*.

Spielberg explained to a crowd during an American Film Institute seminar in late 1973 that a director is "hot" when he's doing his first film. "... if you have a good agent, he'll make your next three deals — before your film comes out. Then, if your film comes out and it crashes ... you've got three films in which to redeem yourself."

Jaws would be the director's chance to redeem himself.

Filmed on location on Martha's Vineyard in early 1974, *Jaws* was a modestly budgeted thriller based on the yet unpublished book by Peter Benchley. Benchley began writing the book in the mid-60s after reading about a Long Island shark fisherman who had harpooned a shark weighing roughly 4,500 pounds.

Spielberg claimed he "stole" the galley proofs off the desk of Richard Zanzuck, one of the heads of Universal. The young director saw it as a fantastic opportunity and wanted to direct the feature, but Spielberg was not what the studio had in mind.

Actually, the project was first turned down by ABC Network Television, which considered it for a TV movie but passed on the deal because they feared it would cost too much to produce. After the success of the hardback book, the publishing industry began battling for the paperback rights and Bantam Books came out on top after reportedly offering $575,000. It was around this time that the idea of a feature film became a reality. If the book could create a stir, a movie could do more.

Once Universal execs caught wind of the book they saw a hit movie and the book began making its rounds. Paul Newman was one of the first actors the studio had in mind for the project. And in the role of director, Alfred Hitchcock was the studio's first choice. Once the film rights were obtained the studio came forth with initial plans of making the feature for a mere $750,000. Some were skeptical that the movie could be made on such a low budget. Filming on water is often the most difficult of locations, but the studio heads believe it could be managed on less than a million dollars. They were wrong.

Hitchcock never materialized as director, so John Sturges and Dick Richards were considered for the director's spot, but when Spielberg expressed his interest the studio took notice. They wanted a film that would really shake up audiences and felt a young director might be able to provide that, and they were impressed enough with his earlier works in TV to believe he could accomplish the task.

For casting, Spielberg wanted little known actors, so no celebrity would cast a shadow over the film. "I wanted somewhat anonymous actors to be in it so you would believe this was happening to you and me," admitted the director. Richard Dreyfuss and Roy Scheider were cast as two of the male leads, along with Robert Shaw, who had recently starred in *The Sting* and was a well-known actor, but not a star. The studio had wanted celebrities like Charlton Heston and Jan Michael Vincent to star in the picture, but the director won out.

Some have described *Jaws* as "the most difficult film ever made." When principle photography began in May 1974 the shooting schedule was set at 55 days. Things began on a bad note when the mechanical shark built to be the star of the film failed to work properly and as time went on things only got worse. The budget began to spiral out of control and the shooting schedule stretched to 159 days.

One of the biggest problems was shooting at sea. Most water features use tanks to shoot key scenes and close-ups so that they have more control over the surroundings. But Spielberg and the producers of the film wanted *Jaws* to be filmed at sea so it would look authentic. However, the aim of realism presented the filmmakers with major difficulties and was one of the main reasons the schedule expanded as much as it did.

The film was said to have started filming without a script or a star — the shark, that is. Initially there was talk of using actual sharks for the entire filming, but soon it became apparent that sharks would not act on cue and a mechanical device would be needed for many of the shots. A giant polythylene gray shark, about 26-feet in length, was designed and named "Bruce" in honor of Spielberg's lawyer, Bruce Ramer.

After six months of grueling pre-production the director began to have second thoughts. "I stayed up at night fantasizing about how I could get myself off this picture short of dying," recalled Spielberg. But the director hung in there.

In May 1974, with a budget of $3.5

million, *Jaws* began filming, but the shark was having trouble. Its jaw would not close properly and the eyes appeared crossed on film. Then on the third day of filming one of the three sharks built for the movie sank and the production crew began affectionately referring to the film as "Flaws." Production was shut down for days while repairs were made to the sharks. Soon the director found the filming behind schedule and the budget climbing. He spent day and night on the set and knew the only way out was to finish the film and succeed, helping the studio make back its money.

In October 1974 location shooting on Martha's Vineyard finally came to a close. What was expected to be a 55-day shoot stretched into a 159-day shoot. And the $3.5 million budget had topped $10 million.

The director thought his career at Universal was over. He was wrong.

On March 26, 1975 *Jaws* had a sneak preview at the Medallion Theater in Dallas. The director stood in back as the movie began, waiting for audience response. The film opened and early on a boy on a raft is killed. Moments later a man jumped from his seat and ran up the aisle out of the theater.

Spielberg thought it was a walk-out and soon everyone would leave the show, but the man got to the lobby and threw up. "That's when I knew we had a hit," the director recalled. Universal opened the film in 400 theaters on June 20, 1975 and it soon was the number one movie across the country. The massive opening was a new idea to the studios and soon became commonplace. The film earned $129 million and soon everyone was afraid of the water.

The monster hit was followed up with numerous sequels, never quite achieving the success of the original, but performing at varying levels of success at the box office. But the combination of disaster and horror became commonplace through the remainder of the decade and Hollywood used every trick it could to create fear — bees, ants, bugs, whales and more — but none caused the stir that *Jaws* had. In fact, unveiled the same summer as *Jaws* was a picture by longtime director William Castle

called *Bug*. *Bug*, in some ways, illustrates the worst the genre had to offer and for once the critics and the fans seemed to agree.

seven
Disaster Meets Horror at the Box Office

Making Moviegoers Squirm

William Castle, unlike Steven Spielberg, had been around Hollywood a long time. Having arrived in Hollywood in the late 1930s, Castle learned about show business as an actor, writer, director and producer. By the 1950s he had had enough of the studio system and stepped out on his own creating campy horror films that drew teen-agers looking for a good scare. His pictures had limited budgets and no stars, so in order to promote the pictures Castle found ingenious gimmicks to create publicity and interest. For *Macabre* he offered life insurance policies against death by fright. For *The Tingler* he placed electric buzzers beneath the seats to shock moviegoers. He tried ghost viewers, flying skeletons, and punishment polls as well. He finally reached his peak in 1968 as producer of *Rosemary's Baby,* the smash horror hit directed by Roman Polanski. After that things went downhill and never would he find that level of success again.

In the early 1970s the horror picture was out of fashion, but in 1973 *The Exorcist* created new interest in the genre and Castle decided to try and get back in the game and never one to pass up on an opportunity, William Castle wanted to ride the tailcoats of the genre once again in hopes of finding a hit. "I felt 1975 would be a big year for me if I could find the right material for a film," he wrote in his memoirs. He recalled hearing about other major pictures in production during that time, including *Earthquake, The Towering Inferno* and *Jaws*, and believed that it would be a frightening year at the movies and he needed to be a part of it.

"I had very little money to work with, and I knew I would be in competition with the multimillion-dollar disaster films the other studios were preparing," said Castle. He was working at Paramount, as he had been since the late 1960s after the success of *Rosemary's Baby*, but his track record was far from solid and the horrific response to his last film *Shanks*, which bombed at the box office, only made his efforts more risky, but in 1974 he found a project and convinced Paramount to let him make the film.

The film is based on Thomas Page's novel *The Hephaestus Plague* and Castle wrote the screenplay himself with the help of Page. He decided a name change was in order. Named after the Greek god of fire, Hephaestus, the title was acceptable for a book, but Castle felt it would never do for a film. He even said that during casting of the picture many of the actors who called about the film would get the name wrong, calling it "The Hepatitis Plague" or "The Hibiscus Plague."

Bug, he decided, was easy to remember, one word, and aptly described what the film would be about. *Bug* tells the story of a small town hit by a strong earthquake that causes an invasion of large bugs that have lived for years deep inside the earth. Living on charred ash, the bugs are capable of starting fires and begin terrorizing the town.

Keeping costs down to a minimum Castle utilized the talents of many people who were working mainly in television. The director, Jeannot Szwarc, had most of his experience on the small screen, having directed shows like *The Rockford Files* and *Columbo*.

The stars of the picture, also had strong experience in TV. Bradford Dillman began in film, winning a Golden Globe award in 1959 as most promising newcomer, but had transitioned into television with a variety TV movie and series appearances on shows like *Columbo*, *Mission Impossible*, *The Night Gallery* and *Mary Tyler Moore*. Joanna Miles started in soap operas like *The Secret Storm*, *The Edge of Night* and *All My Children* and did a variety of other television projects over the years. Others in the cast included Alan Fudge, Richard Gilliland, Jamie Smith Jackson and Patty McCormack, who was best remembered for her starring role in *The Bad Seed*, but also did television work.

But for Castle, the real stars of the film were the bugs and he went to great efforts to cast the perfect creatures.

Castle felt that audiences of the day were

more sophisticated than in the 1950s and he couldn't use mechanical bugs or special effects, but needed the real thing to scare audiences. Someone suggested Ken Middleman, a director of photography at the University of California at Riverside. He had done insect photography for another film, *Hellstrom Chronicles,* and was recommended. Castle contacted him and he arranged to find the proper bugs, which were raised and trained for the film. Getting them to behave may have actually been easier that the actors.

Castle explained in his memoirs that much of the cast and crew were afraid of the bugs and didn't want them crawling on them. Fake bugs were used in some of the scenes with the actors.

Not all scenes made it into the final picture. Castle wrote in his memoirs that MPAA ratings board complained about one of his scenes in which bugs chew an actress' head off and it then rolls onto the kitchen floor. Castle thought teen-agers would love the gore, but the scene never found its way into the movie.

For the final scene, large flying insects were expected to pour from a crack in the earth. Castle couldn't find a bug with red wings that was large enough to create the menacing feel he was hoping for. Middleman managed to make the scene work by shooing common flies with phosphorescent powder on their wings to make them look red. Special effects were used to enlarge the flies so they looked much bigger and Castle was happy with the resulting scene.

The movie begins with James Parmiter, a university scientist, dropping his wife off at church. He leaves for work and she heads to mass when a severe earthquake strikes and townspeople run for cover. Large bugs are released through a huge crack in the earth and begin to menace the small town. They travel in car exhaust pipes because they live on ash and carbon. The bugs release fire from their bottoms and soon fires are exploding cars, setting houses and farms on fire and killing innocent bystanders.

A local student discovers the bugs and brings them to the attention of Parmiter who begins studying them. After his wife is killed by one of the nasty creatures he barricades himself in a small house and begins intense research. His study leads him to mate the bugs with a common cockroach and the bugs then begin reproducing. They also begin to show signs of intelligence, by crawling into formation and spelling out words on the wall like "We Live" and "Parmiter."

Eventually the bugs escape and crawl back into the earth, only to rebirth, but this time flying and finding their way into the house to kill Parmiter. The bugs somehow return to where they came from and another movement of the earth closes the crack, sealing them inside once again and saving the world.

Bug was released to dismal reviews and little box office. Castle, however, had one last gimmick up his sleeve in hopes of drawing some attention to his film. He mounted a large promotional tour for the premiere of *Bug* in a number of U.S. cities. On the tour he brought along one of the stars of the picture, a large bug named Hercules. His promotional gimmick traveled back to his 1958 release of *Macabre* and this time, instead of insuring the audience against death, he insured his bug to the tune of $1 million. If the bug died of natural causes during the promotional tour, excluding any unnatural or violent death, Castle would receive the money.

It was one last publicity stunt, but it didn't help the movie. *Bug* earned terrible reviews and, as Castle had feared, the film found it difficult to compete at the box office among the big budget features released in 1975. While some reviews called the film "weird" and "undeniably stupid," the *New York Times* went a step further when it said "It is not simply a scary picture, nor simply a violent one. It is a cruel picture."

The review went on to say the film "does vile things," and "is sick, and literally sickening." It urged viewers to not go see the movie and analogized it by saying, "If a restaurant reviewer eats a poor meal, that's one thing. If he gets ptomaine poisoning, that's another. *Bug* is decidedly poisonous."

Stephen Farber, another *New York Times*

writer, wrote a blistering criticism of *Jaws* in its release that same year and compared both films. "Both *Jaws* and *Bug* belong to the Pavlov dog school of filmmaking," wrote Farber. "They treat the audience like laboratory animals wired to twitch whenever the electricity is turned on."

But Farber added that while *Bug* was easily recognized as a "cheap exploitation picture" the Steven Spielberg film was an "$8 million exploitation picture."

For Castle, any comparison to the smash horror hit was probably the best he could have hoped for. William Castle died in 1977 and *Bug* was the last film he directed.

eight

It May Be Disaster in the Sky, But Can It Fly?

'Airport' Sequels & Copies

Surprisingly enough, it took several years for Universal to come up with a sequel to the hit feature *Airport*. In reality, sequels were fairly rare in Hollywood even in the early 1970s. *Planet of the Apes* was one of the few Hollywood hits that began producing follow-up features tied to the original hit. Soon all of Hollywood would catch on and almost any hit film would be followed with a sequel, but in 1970 the idea was just beginning to catch on.

Skyjacked

However, in 1972 Hollywood took to the air again with *Skyjacked*. Capitalizing on the success of *Airport*, *Skyjacked* featured another all-star cast with another troubled man trying to take over a plane full of passengers. This time it was a Vietnam bomber demanding to be taken to Russia.

Based on the novel "Hijacked," MGM approached Charleton Heston to star in the picture around April, 1971. After negotiations and a name change, Heston agreed to take the role of the pilot. Heston's deal included a percentage of the film's gross.

Filmed in part at the Metropolitan Oakland International Airport in Oakland, California, the drama/adventure starred Charleton Heston as the Boeing 707's captain, Hank O'Hara. It was Heston's first foray into the disaster genre, but not far from his usual fare. Heston was one of the few longtime leading men from old Hollywood who transitioned well into the Hollywood of the 70s. From his earlier action pictures like *Ben Hur*, Heston moved into the 1970 with hits like *Planet of the Apes* and *The Omega Man*. Following the success of *Skyjacked*, Heston would find himself back in the cockpit a few years later in *Airport 1975*.

Filming on *Skyjacked* actually began in January 1972, but Heston began preparing for the role in late 1971 with him practicing his piloting duties aboard a 707-jet simulator.

Heston claimed he found little challenging about his role in the film, but felt the director's challenge of filming the movie in such a confined space as an airplane presented the difficulties.

For *Skyjacked*, Heston co-starred with Yvette Mimieux, James Brolin, Claude Akins, Susan Dey, Mariette Hartley, Rosie Grier, Walter Pidgeon, Leslie Uggams, John Hillerman, Jeanne Crain and Maureen Connell. John Guillerman, who would go onto make *The Towering Inferno*, directed the film. Heston found the director quite suitable for the film. When production was finished in March, 1972 Heston commented that he thought the movie looked "surprisingly good," and although he expected little acclaim for his lackluster role in the feature he did expect the movie to return a decent profit.

While not as successful as the *Airport* series, *Skyjacked* proved there was longevity in the disaster-type genre, especially in the disaster in the sky feature. The film grossed more than $2.5 million in its first week after opening in May 1972 and topped $5 million in its domestic release before moving onto the worldwide market. The film was, however, banned in Australia when the government decided that its vivid depiction of hijacking methods brought back memories of a airliner bomb hoax in 1971.

Even so, within a year Universal was preparing to take to the skies again and Charleton Heston was once again aboard as a pilot.

Airport 1975

In 1974 the production of a Universal sequel to *Airport* finally got underway. Jennings Lang took over the producer responsibilities for the series after Ross Hunter exited Universal. Lang had produced a number of films at the studio, including *Tell Them Willie Boy Is Here, They Might Be Giants*, and *The Great Northfield Minnesota Raid*. Lang would go on to produce the next three films in the series.

Airport 1975 was released in October, 1974 and starred Karen Black as a stewardess forced to fly a 747 after the crew is killed or injured when a small plane crashes into the cockpit of the jumbo jet, while Charleton Heston, her boyfriend and an ace pilot, tries to talk her through her flying duties. He eventually makes daring attempt to get aboard the plane in flight and save the day. Adding to the drama is a host of co-stars including Efrem Zimbalist Jr. and Erik Estrada, Dana Andrews, Gloria Swanson, Jerry Stiller, Beverly Garland, Chris Norris, Linda Blair, Myrna Loy, Sid Caesar, Susan Clark and, once again, George Kennedy. The film followed the structure and style of the original and was directed by Jack Smight. Co-producing the film was William Frye.

For actress Karen Black it was one of a string of successful roles in the mid-1970s after earning an Oscar nomination and New York Film Critics Award for *Five Easy Pieces* several years earlier. By the mid-70s she was on a hot streak with films like *Day of the Locust*, *The Great Gatsby*, *Capricorn One* and *Family Plot*.

For Heston, he had already taken the lot role for *Skyjacked* and was hard at work on another disaster picture, *Earthquake*, when he was offered the role in *Airport '75*. Heston again found the role lacking, but because his role was small he expected it to only take a few weeks of his time. At the same time, the big-budget feature promised him visibility and profits, so he agreed to take the part. Heston again headed to the flight simulator to prepare for the film, this time he spent his time talking stewardesses through flight procedures, much the way his character would do on the big screen.

Airport 1975 received mixed reviews. Some called the feature laughable while others found it a rehash of the original feature. But the film drew enough fans of the original to succeed at the box office. And while the producers never expected it to reap the rewards of the first feature, they felt the formula would make money. Universal allowed the budget to top out at $4 million and when the feature earned $25.8 million at the domestic box office and nearly $50 million worldwide it became one of the big hits of the year, behind *Blazing Saddles*, *The Godfather Part II*, and two other disaster pictures, *The Towering Inferno* and *Earthquake*. And while the original *Airport* pulled in some $90 million around the globe, its follow-up earned significantly less, but enough to make the studio take notice. The success of the first sequel gave the producers hope that another film could also make money, so shortly after, another film in the series was launched.

Airport '77

Lang and Frye set forth on the next installment of the *Airport* series shortly after the success of *Airport 1975*. This time Jerry Jameson was assigned the directing duties with a story by H.A.L. Craig and Charles Kuenstle. An all-star cast was again selected. This time Jack Lemmon was hired on as the pilot with Brenda Vaccaro as his stewardess/girlfriend. Others on the plane were Lee Grant, Christopher Lee, Joseph Cotton, Olivia De Havilland, Darren McGavin and Pamela Bellwood. George Kennedy was once again on the ground and Jimmy Stewart was assigned the role of Phillip Stevens, owner of the airline. Jennings Lang also had his wife, Monica Lewis, cast in a small role as one of the stewardesses on board, just as he had in *Earthquake*. She would later appear in the final *Airport* installment as well.

This time the story revolves around a luxury jumbo jet flying over the Bermuda Triangle. A collection of VIPs and some priceless art are on board when hijackers drug everyone on the flight with the intent to steal the art. When things goes wrong the plane crashes into the ocean, sinking to the ocean floor. Since the plane is off course and beneath radar, no one can find them and it's up to the pilot and passengers to save themselves before the air runs out.

Again the feature received mixed reviews, but the formidable cast offered memorable performances and the story actually kept the series from becoming too stale. Even so, *The Washington Post* wrote after the film's release in March 1977, "In Airport '77, the new installment of a series Universal has threatened to continue for a generation, the writers simply give up trying to sustain airborne peril; they vary the formula by dropping the plane in the ocean, so that it becomes a sunken airship."

Star Jack Lemmon, several months after the release of the film told *U.S. News & World Report* that filmmaking "isn't as much fun" anymore, adding that economic pressures created by television made Hollywood less willing to take chances on small, worthwhile projects. Instead, sex and violence were the staples behind the few major films put out by the Hollywood studios. While he never directly referred to his experience on *Airport '77*, it was apparent that the film, which some felt was a waste of his talent, was not one of the features he was most proud of.

Even so, *Airport '77* took in nearly $30 million worldwide and was found more credible with the critics than its predecessor, *Airport 1975*. On the release of *Airplane!*, Hollywood's spoof of the disaster in the air series, one reviewer wrote, "Though it obviously aims to be sassy and uninhibited, *Airplane!* never approaches the comic heights achieved unwittingly by *Airport 1975* and the peerless *Concorde — Airport 1979*.

Concorde — Airport 1979

Once again, by scaling back on costs and reducing expectations, Jennings Lang and co-producer William Frye launched the next film in the series shortly after *Airport '77* was released.

By this time, television had caught onto the disaster in the air theme and TV movies like *Mayday at 40,000* and *Death Flight SST* were crowding the airways, so not only was the series losing steam on the big screen, but the little screen was offering the same entertainment and not charging a price of admission.

For the big screen, though, Lang hired director David Lowell Rich whose experience was primarily in television, making movies like *Death Flight SST* and *Telethon*, to direct the feature. This time, the new Concorde jet was the talk in travel, promising international flights with domestic travel times. With a worldwide release the film had several different titles, including *Airport '80: The Concorde, The Concorde Affair*, and *S.O.S. Concorde*.

For this outing Robert Wagner and Susan Blakely, the stars of *The Towering Inferno*, took on the leading roles and George Kennedy, who normally stayed on the ground for the *Airport* series, found himself helping pilot the plane, but reprising his role of Joe Petroni. The all-star cast was growing weaker with Sylvia Kristel,

Eddie Albert, Bibi Anderson, Charo, John Davidson, Andrea Marcovicci, Martha Raye, Alan Delon, Cicely Tyson, Jimmie Walker and Mercades McCambridge taking over many of the supporting roles.

Location shooting in late 1978 brought some of the cast to Dulles Airport, with other shooting taking place in Hollywood and the film was released in mid-1979. The premise had Blakely as a TV news reporter uncovering secret information that could ruin a wealthy industrialist, played by Wagner. Wagner then sets off on trying to crash the plane, destroying both Blakely and the evidence she has against him.

The film earned poor reviews and found little interest at the box office. The vast number of disaster in the air features had begun to bore the public and the themes and formulas were so exhausted that *The Concorde — Airport 1979* failed at the box office and brought an end to the *Airport* series.

Another Airport?

But, producer Jennings Lang was unwilling to let the series die. In 1983 he announced plans for another Universal feature called *Airport 2000*. The feature was supposed to take place in the future and again would star George Kennedy.

Writer, director Larry Cohen was assigned the task of writing the screenplay and Lang promised that the feature would again have an all-star cast and contain the elements that made the earlier features successful, but would also take the series into the future with space travel. The film, however, never got off the ground.

Air Disasters Continue

But disaster and danger in the sky has continued to be a popular subject at the movies and in the years since, a number of films have carried on the tradition, hoping to combine action, suspense and disaster into big box office dollars. Some have succeeded more than others, but all pay tribute to Universal's *Airport* series.

Bruce Willis' *Die Hard II* had terrorists taking over an airport, bringing deadly results with plane crashes, explosions and a plane of frightened passengers, including Willis' onscreen wife, Bonnie Bedelia. *Passenger 57* put Wesley Snipes on board a hijacked flight as a cop who is the only hope for a plane full of passengers.

Other films featuring terror in the skies include *Turbulence, Con-Air, Executive Decision*, *Airforce One*, *Red Eye* and to a lesser extent, *Hero* starring Dustin Hoffman, and *Fearless* with Jeff Bridges. Even Jodie Foster got in the act in 2005 with her big screen air drama, *Flightplan*.

nine

Taking the Sting out of the Disaster Movie

Irwin Allen Gets Stung

After producing big screen hits like *The Poseidon Adventure* and *The Towering Inferno*, Irwin Allen earned new clout in Hollywood. While the films were not critically acclaimed, they reaped reward at the box when the two features took in nearly $100 million combined.

Allen's disaster features also earned several Oscar nods and were applauded for their special effects, all-star casts and action sequences earning them a place in cinematic history for their effects, casts of stars and glamour.

In 1978, Allen followed up his successes with another disaster, but this time he avoided flood and fire and looked skyward. While the *Airport* features had succeeded at the box office by placing disaster in the air, Allen chose a different method of mayhem. Much closer to Alfred Hitchcock's 1963 film, *The Birds*, Allen saw an attack by killer bees as a disaster waiting to happen. *The Swarm* was the result.

Hoping For Another Hit

While Allen handed the directing duties of *The Poseidon Adventure* off entirely to Ronald Neame, and only directed the action sequences in *The Towering Inferno*, for *The Swarm* he oversaw the direction of the entire picture. He also assembled a starring cast to rival his earlier efforts. This time Michael Caine accepted the leading role with Katharine Ross at his side. Richard Widmark, Henry Fonda, Fred MacMurray, Patty Duke, Jose Ferrer and Bradford Dillman also filled out the cast. In addition, Olivia de Havilland, who passed on an opportunity to star in *The Towering Inferno*, this time accepted a co-starring role in the Irwin Allen production.

The film hoped to capitalize on real fears and concerns about African killer bees, as the subject had already been discussed in the press and the possibility that the bees could one day find their way into the United States was already under debate. It was reported that in 1956, 26

African killer bees escaped from a laboratory in Brazil. No one knew how violent the bees could be, how large the swarm might grow or how far the danger could spread. However, there had been a number of deaths attributed to the bees in South America in the years that followed, but the bees reportedly had not advanced into Central America and none had ever been identified in the United States.

Allen's feature theorized that the bees made their way into Texas where they infiltrate a military base, killing everyone inside. As the feature begins, military personnel are descending upon the base to uncover the fate of the people there. When two military helicopters crash after encountering the bees, the authorities begin to fear the worst. Michael Caine, a scientist tracking the bees, is placed in charge of a unit to destroy the bees and save the country, while his military counterparts, played by Richard Widmark and Bradford Dillman, disagree with his approach to solving the dilemma and opt to work against him as much as they do the bees. Katharine Ross, a military doctor, takes Caine's

side and the two begin a romance.

Meanwhile, a nearby town preparing for a flower festival, becomes the next scene of destruction as townspeople are attacked by angry bees, obviously bent on death and destruction. The town is evacuated, but when the bees attack the train carrying the townspeople away, the conductor is killed and the train flies off its tracks killing everyone aboard.

The bees then head for Houston with the military and the scientist trying various approaches for stopping the bees. Houston is evacuated and the city is burned to hopefully kill the bees with the fire. The effort again fails and the bees find their way into the military headquarters killing Widmark, Dillman and all other opposition to Caine. Caine, however, discovers a sound frequency that draws the bees and in a last-ditch effort, places buoys producing the sound in the nearby bay with an oil slick surrounding them. Once the bees are drawn to the sound, landing on the water and oil surface, Caine and the few military personnel who are still alive, set the oil on fire killing the bees and saving the rest of the United States.

Promoting the Film

The film reportedly cost $11.5 million to produce, along with another $7.3 million to market and promote, topping out at nearly $19 million. To promote the picture Allen and Warner Bros. used an ingenious way to obtain media coverage. They highlighted the film as the season's biggest Hollywood movie that everyone was talking about and produced a documentary called *Inside The Swarm*, which took viewers behind the scenes of the feature and the danger of the real killer bees. Allen got 72 U.S. TV stations to air his "documentary," resulting in free publicity for his film. "If we had to buy the time on 72 stations, it would cost us $5.5 million," Allen said in an interview at the time. "The TV stations sell spots on the documentary and make a fortune. Everybody wins."

The Swarm opened at 1,400 theaters across the nation on July 14, 1978. It was one of the largest openings ever. The reviews were not good and it's possible the studio feared this and opted for the wide opening, hoping to draw box office dollars early, before word of mouth kept people from spending their dollars to see the feature.

Apparently, they were right. *Newsweek* wrote, "It may be a little early, but it's probably safe to nominate *The Swarm* for the worst movie of the year. Taken, as they say from today's headlines, this cheap-jack combo horror-disaster by producer-director Irwin Allen speculates on what could happen if the African killer bees should cross the Rio Grande. According to Allen, they'd attack a tiny Texas town overpopulated by grand old Hollywood stars, killing most of them instantly and driving the rest into hallucinatory madness.

The Washington Post, on the other hand, said the film did "manage to turn the industrious little honeybee into a menace so seemingly convincing that America may go bee-crazy this summer," but also added "... Allen has coaxed better performances from the 22 million bees he used in the film than from most of his actors."

The film fared poorly at the box office. Warner Bros. even predicted the film would earn only about $10-$12 million in its release. Actually, in May 1977, several months before the film's release Warner Bros. market research division conducted a study and released an internal report entitled, "An Exploratory Study of Marketing Opportunities for *The Swarm*." The report found below-average interest from moviegoers toward seeing the film and indicated the features main problem was "a general failure of moviegoers to recognize that the killer bee menace is real."

The report also found that the public was beginning to find disaster films "increasingly stereotyped" and that the film closely resembled other features on television or in movie theaters. The latter was certainly true. In fact, *Bug*, by William Castle had been released and failed in 1975 and *The Bees*, a Mexican production chronicling a similar story of an attack by African killer bees was also due in theaters in 1978. Another feature on TV, this time involving ants, and a film about piranhas, also had similarities to *The Swarm*.

With the information uncovered in the report, Warner Bros. had to decide the best method for releasing the picture. In August, 1977, a year before the film's release, the studio sent brochures to exhibitors telling them about the upcoming film, describing it as "what we hope to be the greatest adventure-survival movie of all time" and highlighting Allen for his production successes in *The Poseidon Adventure* and *The Towering Inferno*.

In December, 1977 the studio advertised in *Boxoffice* magazine and sent out more brochures to exhibitors, this time calling the film "your summer of '78 blockbuster ... a chilling, riveting, harrowing, cinematic experience."

Normally, film exhibitors are given an opportunity to view all or portions of a film prior to bidding on an opportunity to screen the picture. However, in the case of *The Swarm*, Warner Bros. took blind bids, meaning the exhibitors had to bid for a chance to show the picture without ever seeing any of it. All they had to go on was promotion from the studio that the film would be a "blockbuster" and promises that the film would be as successful as the director's previous efforts. Marketing material compared the movie to *The Poseidon Adventure*, which took in $42 million, and to *The Towering Inferno*, which took in $50 million. But *The Swarm* was a bust, earning $10 million in its release.

Theater owners were not happy with the result and Presidio Enterprises, Inc., a company owning several Texas theaters filed suit against Warner Bros. for deceptive trade practices. In the suit the theater owner claimed that the studio knew the problems facing the picture, which were chronicled in the marketing report, but held back the information, promising the movie would be a blockbuster because of Allen's previous hits. And then the studio made matters worse by telling the theater chain the film could not be screened before the bid deadline. Presidio's bid for the film was accepted by Warner Bros., but the film lost money for the company. Filed in 1979, the lawsuit took several years for the court case to work itself out. In October, 1984 *Entertainment Law Reporter* wrote that Federal District Court found in favor of the theater owner and awarded them more than $520,000 in damages because Warner Bros. violated the state's Deceptive Trade Practices and Consumer Protection Act.

One interesting footnote to the story is that in 1990 the news media reported that African killer bees had now crossed the Rio Grande and were at last in the United States. The publicity resulted in a surge in popularity for the film in its video release as the public began renting the feature to find out what disaster might be in store.

ten
The Disaster Picture Begins Losing Steam

93

The Demise of the Genre

By 1978 the disaster picture was no longer of interest to the movie going public. As illustrated with the failure of Irwin Allen's *The Swarm* and several other pictures, the public was no longer plunking down its ticket money for a disaster. And while it's difficult to find the underlying factors in the demise of the disaster genre at this point, Hollywood has generally found itself caught in cycles where various genres and styles of filmmaking are in fashion and of interest to moviegoers, but in time those genres fade and a new one takes over.

The early 1970s found the disaster picture in style perhaps because of the state of the country's psyche. After the assassinations and war of the 1960s and the government cover-ups and conspiracies that enveloped the nation, the disaster picture, some suggest, seemed an escape because they placed the enemy outside of our control, and in many respects, in Mother Nature. Man was often at fault for not paying attention or using greed to get ahead, but it was always "an act of God" that caught us off guard. Others said that man's greed and ignorance led to the wrath of Mother Nature.

When the disaster genre began to fade the country was evolving away from the scandal and tragedies and was facing an economic crisis and expanding world turmoil that possibly made the disasters seem closer to home. It appears, the genre that succeeded most after the demise of the disaster picture, was the horror film. The 1980s saw a resurgence of the slasher film, which drew teen-agers looking for blood and gore and a body count.

But in the later part of the 1970s the disaster picture had seen the grand successes of *Airport, The Poseidon Adventure* and *Towering Inferno*. The attention these films and several others drew, had Hollywood trying to find every possible angle to the disaster and to capture it on film, hoping to lure moviegoers and find

95

the box office attention the earlier features had found. But in order to achieve this the studios found that there were two paths to go in order for success. The first was to invest more to make the epic larger-than-life, by hiring bigger stars and investing more in special effects. Several later films, including *Swarm* and *Meteor*, were some of the most expensive disaster pictures to date, averaging in at roughly $20 million by the time they hit theaters. The filmmakers approaching the genre this way believed that this was the only way to achieve the attention to create the "event picture" that earlier films had achieved with less.

The second method of approach was to capitalize on the success of an original by copying the style and formula of a hit, but to do it on less money. This approach most always resulted in less box office success, but reduced costs helped make these films profitable. The *Airport* series is possibly the best example of this type of filmmaking. Each *Airport* film found a tighter budget to create the film, but because they were tying into a previous hit, the producers felt they had a built-in audience and at least a large

percentage of fans of the previous film would turn out to see another in the series. Irwin Allen approached this method himself with *Beyond The Poseidon Adventure*. But with both approaches the public was still needed to decide the success or failure of each film and by the later 1970s it appeared that few were still interested in the disaster picture.

Avalanche

New World Pictures jumped onto the disaster picture bandwagon in 1978 with the release of *Avalanche*, starring Rock Hudson and Mia Farrow. Roger Corman, best known for his low-budget horror pictures of the 1960s, was the owner of the production company and hoped to create mayhem with snow and ice.

Filmed on location in parts of Colorado, using the Rockies as a backdrop, the story has Hudson building a fabulous ski resort in a remote area. He invites famous skiers, skaters and anyone else he can think of, including his ex-wife, played by Farrow, to the resort's grand opening. When a small plane crashes into a mountaintop it causes an avalanche of snow and ice to come pounding down on the resort and anyone in its path.

While the premise sounds solid, the resulting feature failed to interest moviegoers. The limited budget was spent on hiring the talents of Hudson and Farrow, while the remaining cast was of little notoriety or talent. And even so, little money was left over for the effects that were required to make the film work.

One reviewer said the Hudson and Farrow were competing for the title of who could look worst on skis and that Hudson won. Hudson himself said he accepted the role mainly for the money, but that he was sorry he did. "It was an el cheapo. I thought no one would see it."

Another reviewer said the film was "basically a marvel of disorganized exposition and cut-rate disaster effects," and wondered whether someone actually decided to set out to make a disaster at a ski resort in the Rockies or whether Corman simply had ski footage lying around and decided to make a movie out of it.

The disaster footage was said to be "faked so poorly that there never appears to be a pictorial connection between the rampaging snow — sometimes falling down real mountains at other times down miniature sets or in tacky optical shots — and the sites and characters it's supposed to pulverize."

While inexpensive to make, compared to most of the other pictures of its day, *Avalanche* sank at the box office and has been called one of the worst of the disaster genre.

Hurricane

Dino De Laurentiis found some success on the big screen in 1976 with his remake of *King Kong*. Starring Jessica Lange and Jeff Bridges, the film used modern day special effects to update the screen classic and moviegoers were drawn to the adventure mainly for its real star — the giant ape. So, several years later De Laurentiis decided to remake another 1930s classic on a grand scale. This time John Ford's 1937 film *The Hurricane*, which starred Dorothy Lamour, would serve as the subject of his next effort.

The producer invested $20 million in the production and hired Jan Troell, whose arlier films included *The Emigrants* and *The New Land*, to direct the feature. For stars, the producers hired Mia Farrow, Max Von Sydow, Jason Robards, and Hawaiian surfer Dayton Ka'ne. De Laurentiis built a $4.5 million resort on the remote island of Bora Bora to house cast and crew during productions and spent lavishly to have imported beef and some 16,000 bottles of wine brought in to make the home away from home more comfortable for cast and crew.

Filming proved to be a challenge, with a laundry list of troubles hitting production. Mia Farrow originally accepted the part when Roman Polanski was assigned as director. Rumors that Farrow and Polanski had an affair during her stay in London and hoped to continue the liaison during filming in the tropical locale. When Polanski was brought down by scandal for having sex with a minor, he bowed out of the production.

In any event, Farrow brought her children with her for the production and while she worked they entertained themselves playing in the sun and sea. Farrow, by contrast, spent a great deal of time waste-deep in a tank of salt water to film the 18-minute climactic finale for the feature. And during one scene she was injured after she was thrown against the side of a lifeboat during night filming of the simulated hurricane. The crew of Italians reportedly clashed with locally-hired crewmembers and created trouble on set as well, and electricity was said to come and go causing production delays. Then, sewage from the "hastily built hotel" began to pollute the lagoon where filming was taking place. And to top it off, Mia Farrow's marriage to Andre Previn, which was already on shaky ground, according to Farrow, was reportedly "washed out" after she became involved with the film's cinematographer Sven Nykvist. During filming of one of the disaster's key scenes, the screenwriter was heard to remark, "We could wipe out all the actors in this scene. Not pretend. Really wipe them out."

In the end, however, it was the film that was wiped out.

The feature was supposed to revolve around a love story between Farrow and a young island chieftain, played by Ka'ne, and the trouble created by Farrow's father, played by Robards, and the inevitable hurricane that hits the island at the end of the picture. Critics said Farrow looked too old for the role and that the romance looked ridiculous. The cinematography was called "myopic" and "woozy," while the music was called "piddling" and made up of "broken guitars and warped pianos."

After the film was previewed, *The Hollywood Reporter* wrote that 13 minutes of the film was cut from the picture to try and save the release from failing at the box office. However, the cutting wasn't enough to save the picture and the film never earned back the production costs, pulling in only a reported $5 million at the box office.

Beyond The Poseidon Adventure

In 1978, even with the poor showing of *Swarm*, producer/director Irwin Allen still had not given up on his disaster films. In an August 1978 interview with the *New York Times*, Irwin scoffed at critics who called the genre dead and said the "death of the disaster movie is premature."

For Allen, even with the genre showing serious signs of decline he had several more features planned for the big screen. And at the time of the interview he was in production with *Beyond The Poseidon Adventure*.

The Poseidon Adventure had started Allen's success with the genre and earned him both fame and fortune. And with movie sequels becoming more and more popular by the late 1970s, Allen surely figured a return to his first hit disaster movie might jumpstart the genre and his success rate. Although sequels have rarely equaled the success of their originals, many had found financial rewards far beyond their costs. The *Star Wars* series was finding just beginning to find great success at the time and *Jaws* was spawning several films as well. In addition, the James Bond series, as well as the return of *Airport, Superman, The Omen* and *The Exorcist* all showed that Hollywood had a love of recapturing the success of an original. Allen only hoped *Beyond The Poseidon Adventure* could do half as well as the original.

99

Written by Nelson Gidding and directed by Allen, the film takes up where the original left off. Apparently after the original survivors were rescued from the ship two teams of scavengers arrive on the scene looking to go aboard the S.S. Poseidon in search of wealth. The first crew, led by Michael Caine, is made up on Caine, Sally Field and Karl Malden, and is looking for jewels and cash left behind by the passengers, while the second team, with Telly Savalas and a team of henchmen, is on board to retrieve a stash of plutonium for building a nuclear device.

The two teams split up with Caine's group coming across a band of passengers left alive and still looking for a way out. Slim Pickens, Shirley Jones, Mark Harmon, Peter Boyle, Jack Warden, Shirley Knight, Veronica Hamel and Angela Cartwright look to Caine to save the day. After more dangerous travel through the up-side-down ship, and some rough exchanges with Savalas and his henchmen, the group finally manages to escape the ship.

The picture received mixed reviews. Called inferior to the original, which also earned mixed reviews, the *Washington Post* said the film "has everything except real people in real situations." The film failed to interest moviegoers and the mediocre reviews didn't help. The film went down as one of Allen's failures and did little to breathe new life into the genre. In fact, the glut of poor disaster films, covering every known calamity to man spread the genre so thin that the public began to lose all interest in any type of disaster whatsoever. But there would be several more costly films before the genre would come to a close.

eleven

The 70s Disaster Picture Comes to an End

'Meteor' Crashes & Burns

J ust as the decade of the 1970s dawned a new age for the disaster film, the decade came to a close taking with it the genre that it had, in many ways, given birth to. Book-ending the decade were possibly the genre's greatest hit and its greatest failure. Although the disaster film didn't actually end with the closing of the 70s, its demise was imminent.

The Genre Loses Steam

Airport cost Universal roughly $10 million - a costly sum at the time - but the studio was rewarded with a domestic box-office draw of more than $45 million after the film's release in 1970. In many ways, the release of this film launched the decade of the disaster movie and several noteworthy hits, including several

Airport sequels, followed. But in 1979 the public's interest in the entertainment of disaster was waning. Hollywood, however, failed to take notice and continued churning out films like Beyond the Poseidon Adventure, Swarm and Airport 79. But the films failed to command the attention or the box-office returns their predecessors had. And one of the last features to be released that decade, while spectacular in concept and star power, finally helped to signal the end of the genre - or so we thought. The film was Meteor.

Meteor was an American International Pictures epic that culled the talents of a wide variety of Hollywood names — both in front of and behind the cameras. But the resulting picture, for a variety of reasons, failed miserably and after so many disaster misses, the public lost interest in the genre and the failure was so great that Hollywood finally had no choice but to notice.

A production team of noteworthy success assembled for the making of Meteor. Apparently producer Gabriel Katzka was one of

103

the main forces behind the development of the project. Katzka was a television, theater and film producer whose work included *The Taking of Pelham One, Two, Three; Marlowe; Who'll Stop the Rain* and countless other projects. He was well known around the world for his ability to raise money for producing his projects and it was reportedly those talents that enabled him to pull together the exciting list of players and the money to produce *Meteor*. Fellow producers Samuel Z. Arkoff, Sandy Howard and Sir Run Run Shaw joined forces to produce the picture and hired Ronald Neame, director of *The Poseidon Adventure*, to direct the film. A budget of $17 million promised a first rate picture and the producers promised a cast that would rival that of any disaster film to date.

Stars Sign on to Production

Signed on as star of the picture, Sean Connery, best known for his James Bond action adventures agreed to star in the feature at a salary that was reportedly in the "high six figures." The star was also a friend of Stanley Mann, who wrote the screenplay. In addition to Connery, Natalie Wood, Brian Keith, Karl Malden, Trevor Howard and Henry Fonda accepted roles as major players at hefty star salaries. An extensive supporting cast as well as a large cast of extras was hired to fill out the production. Salaries alone reportedly ate up a large chunk of the budget.

Location shooting promised spectacular visual effects like an avalanche in the Swiss Alps, a tidal wave in China, and the destruction of New York City after an asteroid strike. Producers planned to put at least $3 million of the total budget into the effects alone. And while star power often was the selling factor of an event movie like most standard disaster pictures of the day, special effects were needed to wow an audience so word of mouth would promise continued box-office draw to help a picture succeed. Films like *The Poseidon Adventure* and *The Towering Inferno* succeeded for those reasons. *Meteor* hoped to do the same.

The film opens with a space-age prologue about the universe being an infinite playground for the comet and the danger zone known as the asteroid belt. The credits appear in bold yellow and larger-than-life soaring through space in the fashion of *Superman*, except instead of the words flowing forward in space towards us, the words appear up close and are drawn backwards farther and farther until they disappear into space. When the film actually begins we're introduced to Sean Connery as a former NASA director who's being called back to Washington after a comet hits a large asteroid named Orpheus and knocks the object out of its orbit setting the five-mile chunk of rock on a collision course with Earth.

Connery's character apparently helped design a nuclear warhead satellite to handle just such a dilemma except the government found it more useful in space pointed directly at the Russians. In anger, Connery quits, going off to race his yacht, and NASA now needs Connery to come back to help them realign the satellite to blast apart the comet.   Complicating matters are the facts that not only do they have less than a week to do this, but also that the warheads won't be enough to do the job and that the United States needs Russia's help because they too have a similar weapon aimed at the United States and it would take the combined power of both weapons to destroy Orpheus.

Brian Keith portrays the Russian astrophysicist assigned to work with NASA, while Natalie Wood stars as his translator, and both arrive in the United States to discuss options for joining forces against Orpheus.

Several smaller asteroids that broke off Orpheus in its initial collision with the comet do come crashing through the Earth's atmosphere, causing an earthquake in Siberia, an avalanche in the Swiss Alps, a tidal wave in China and eventually a direct hit on New York City.

Coincidentally, the major players in the film are operating out of a satellite communications facility underneath New York City when the smaller asteroid hits Manhattan causing massive destruction. Explosions and fire reminiscent of *The Towering Inferno*, crashing buildings like in *Earthquake*, and a flooded fate similar to the cast of *The Poseidon Adventure*, have the stars struggling for survival while they wait to see if their plan to blow up Orpheus succeeds. In the end the plan works and the world is saved from destruction.

A Disaster in the Making

Production of the film began in mid-1977 with great promise. Director Ronald Neame was characterized as "impossible to dislike and easy to trust." Location shooting took place in a variety of locales, including New York City, Washington D.C., Switzerland, Hong Kong and several other spots. No major problems were reported during shooting, although one minor problem on the set surrounded the leading lady.

Natalie Wood was approached to star as a Russian translator because she was the only major leading lady in Hollywood who actually new the language because she was raised the daughter of Russian immigrants. Wood apparently wanted to look her best during production, but early on in shooting Wood was told that Neame wanted her to wear less makeup. She reportedly agreed to take some of the make-up off, but it wasn't enough for Neame and he again requested she remove more eye makeup

because he felt she was still wearing too much mascara. Wood replied angrily, "Tell him I'd be happy to wear less makeup, but only if Sean will work without his toupee."

Even with the minor flare-up production continued. The major destruction of New York City shooting took place in Hollywood when a subway station was constructed on a huge water tank that was once used for memorable musicals set on water and starring Esther Williams. The set was flooded with a messy mixture of a water and mud as the script called for. Wood recalled the filming as "being buried alive in a Mix-master. There were over a million gallons of mud in holding containers overhead. As we swam, it came breaking through the ceiling and flying in all directions. You literally couldn't see or hear or say anything. The mud got in our eyes and mouths. The only protection we had was earplugs."

Production on the film ended later in the year and post-production took over. Special effects work took longer than expected, reportedly because the producers faced money troubles and had to find inexpensive ways to make the meteor disaster look real. "We shot the entire movie without the special effects and then they ran out of money and they had all sorts of problems and the special effects were kind of — nothing — I mean, really pathetic — that it never really had a chance," recalled Sean Connery.

But even with the poor special effects the producers had invested too much to not follow through with a release, so an extensive advertising and promotion program was developed to promote the film and the star names attached to the project were used to draw moviegoers. After advertising and promotion costs were added to the production budget the cost of the picture reportedly exceeded $35 million.

A Fantastic Premiere

The premiere of the picture was finally held on October 12, 1979 and the producers felt they had a surefire way to promote the film. The premiere was held at the bottom of the 570-foot crater in Arizona. A red carpet was rolled out and waiters served Meteor beer from France to attendees who were flown down into the crater, which is located about 40 miles outside of Flagstaff, Arizona. Stars, press and VIPs were flown in and given quilted vinyl Meteor jackets, turtleneck sweaters and hats with the movie logo on them, posters and books about meteorites.

Publicity director for the film, Ronni Chasen, told reporters the expensive film required a large investment in promotion. "If a movie is a hit in the U.S., it's likely to be all over the world. America has the most difficult audiences — it's pace-setting." Producer Arkoff said, "We in the distribution end have to provide the razzle-dazzle these days. In the old days, the local theatrical exhibitor did most of that. Now he puts all his razzle-dazzle into the candy counter. So we've got to get out and sell the public ourselves."

The premiere alone reportedly cost the studio more than $3 million.

But all the promotion in the world couldn't save *Meteor*. The movie bombed when it hit the big screen. The *Washington Post* said "Clunk - That's the sound of *Meteor* settling in at area theaters. It makes more noise than the usual disaster film only because more money was spent to sink it."

Other reviews called the movie a "ragged turkey" and "embarrassing." And *Newsweek* wrote, "Director Ronald Neame, who once made good movies, has instructed his actors to shout as much as possible. The rest is special effects — and not very special ones at that."

The major factor in the failure of *Meteor* was simply the poor quality of the special effects. Word of mouth killed the feature because the meteor itself looked like what some called, "a pet rock." And because of the huge success of *Star Wars*, just two years earlier, the level of space-age effects had been increased. *Star Wars* cost roughly $10.5 million and took in more than $185 million in its initial release. The quality of the effects drew fans and set the stage for more space epics utilizing new methods in filmmaking. *Meteor,* however, uses matte paintings and miniatures for most of its special effects, which had been used for years and came across looking dated and inferior. Reviewers

and the public took notice.

With the failure of *Meteor* came the end of the big-budget disaster picture. However, Irwin Allen already had his last theatrical disaster picture in the works and it would be released in 1980. By then the genre was at death's door and his film would do little to save it.

twelve

Time Runs Out on the Disaster Picture

One Last Failure

W hen the disaster movie dawned in 1970 there was a distinct formula that made the genre successful. Those that used the formula well combined elements of drama, suspense, comic relief and adventure with adequate special effects, and were met with warm reception at the box office. But of all the elements, the strongest element behind the success of the 1970s disaster film was the all-star cast.

There were several reasons behind the use of the all-star cast. The first and most obvious reason was the value behind the celebrity. Stars add luster to a film simply by attaching their name to it. Financers are often more willing to invest in a film if a star name is attached to the picture. The credibility a bankable star often gives assurance that a film is of quality and will draw moviegoers to the movie house, returning profits to the investors.

The bankability of a star name is one of the easiest ways to draw interest in a movie. In addition to the fan interest and credibility stars bring to films, they also garner media attention and publicity that might otherwise be unavailable to a film.

But a star name only goes so far. In the end, the film sinks or swims on its own after it premieres at the theater. Star power may draw initial fans to a film, but word of mouth and reviews are the only way to ensure lasting success at the box office. If story, directing and effects don't hold up the promises touted by a film's promotion and advertising, the result will be a short run on the big screen and a poorly viewed film that may tarnish the image of the stars that lend their names to it.

The other, less obvious, reason for utilizing celebrities in the disaster picture is the character development they bring to a film. While this might sound confusing, the reality is that disaster films are built on the adventure, suspense and drama surrounding a major calamity, whether it be natural or man-made. This often means that characters play second fiddle to the special effects and drama in the script. Characters are usually poorly developed and given varying lengths of screen time and their main reason for existing is to further the disaster and show its impact on the people it comes into contact with.

That's not to say that the characters in the disaster film don't have other traumas to deal with, often they do, but the standard disaster picture only has so much time to develop numerous characters before disaster strikes. And since disaster in general must hit a number of people to be considered a major disaster, we need many characters to be affected. But with so little time and so many characters the films have a challenge to create characters the audience will care about in short order to spend the remainder of the time watching them struggle to survive the disaster that's brought down on them.

Because of this, star power plays a key role. Celebrities, by definition, are well known. The public has definite ideas about what celebrities are like, often placing them in high regard. Interest in their lives is intense and relationships are developed that last for years as moviegoers watch celebrity lives unfold on the big or small screen. When introducing them in a disaster picture, character development can be immediate. We already care about the star and want them to survive the disaster they face and the character they play may be irrelevant.

It's often impossible for the screen character and the real celebrity to be separated, and we as viewers find it difficult to distinguish where the star ends and the character begins. But in the disaster picture, that problem is turned into an advantage. We want Paul Newman and Faye Dunaway to survive at the end of *The Towering Inferno*, even though we know very little about whom they are or their relationship before we meet them at the beginning of the picture. The same goes for Shelly Winters in *The Poseidon Adventure*, or Olivia De Havilland in *Airport '77*, or Dean Martin and Jacqueline Bissett in *Airport*. And if they perished we felt affected.

The 1970s Come to an End

The 1970s was a banner decade for the disaster picture and the all-star cast, but by the end of the decade the films were becoming less than spectacular, as were the all-star casts. Several notable failures, including *The Swarm, Hurricane* and *Meteor* showed that the genre was showing signs of decline. Star names were still a major factor in getting the films made in the first place, but the stars themselves were in part responsible for the decline in the quality of the films. Star salaries began to climb throughout the 1970s because the old studio system that kept things in line for decades, crumbled in the 1960s and ushered in a new era where stars were no longer under contract to a studio. No longer were annual salaries or multi-picture deals the norm. Now, stars were often hired on a project-by-project basis and the studios and producers were bidding for the stars to attach themselves to a particular project. Stars began to realize their value to the success of a film and began expecting larger salaries and cuts of the profits of the films they made.

For disaster pictures, star names were often the draw that created interest in the films and the expense of hiring the name talent began to get so high that often other areas of the production, mainly set design and special effects were sacrificed. The result was a lot of wasted talent with hokey, and sometimes laughable, effects that were magnified on the big screen and the terrible reviews that followed began to reflect on the entire genre.

Films like *Beyond the Poseidon Adventure, Avalanche* and *The Concorde - Airport 1979* were giving the genre a bad name because poor scripts and mediocre effects gave the public little to follow or find interesting. Except for the star names in these pictures, like Rock Hudson, Mia Farrow, Michael Caine, Sally Field and Robert Wagner, the films had little to offer.

By the close of the decade the genre had seen nothing but several years of failures, and expensive ones at that. However, in 1980 Irwin Allen had one more shot at success and used his clout in Hollywood to make a picture that he hoped would recapture his illustrious past and rejuvenate the genre that had made him rich and famous.

When Time Ran Out

After the failures of his last few films, Allen had actually told reporters he was getting out of the disaster movie business. Even so, sometime in 1979, Allen entered into a deal with Warner Bros. to produce a film about a disastrous erupting volcano and the band of people caught in its path. The volcano epic, as discussed earlier, was not an uncommon one, and, in fact, was one of the original and most common of disaster vehicles. However, since the dawning of the full-fledged disaster picture in 1970, no volcanoes had erupted on the big screen.

Allen must have been convinced the concept would succeed at the box office and gathered another all-star cast, as well as a budget of $20 million, for his disaster epic. Based on the novel *The Day the World Ended* by Gordon Thomas and Max Morgan Witts, Allen once again used screenwriter Sterling Silliphant,

along with the help of Carl Foreman, to produce the screenplay. And while Allen himself had been at the helm of directing duties for his last two failures, *Swarm* and *Beyond the Poseidon Adventure*, he hired James Goldstone as director of the film that he retitled *When Time Ran Out*. Goldstone's previous directing credits included *Calamity Jane*, as well as the TV series *Star Trek*, and he was not entirely new to the disaster genre either. In 1977, Goldstone directed *Rollercoast*, a quasi-disaster/suspense film about and extortionist planting bombs on roller coasters at popular amusement parks. The film even had an all-star cast that included Timothy Bottoms, George Segal, Richard Widmark, Susan Strasberg and Henry Fonda, as mentioned earlier.

It's Another All-Star Cast

To ensure success Allen pulled together another all-star cast of celebrities. He clung to the tried and true and hired a group of actors who had fared well in a number of disaster pictures already. Paul Newman was again brought in at his million-dollar salary after having made it through *The Towering Inferno* roughly six years earlier. Newman admitted in and interview several years later that his primary reason for accepting the role in *When Time Ran Out,* was the money, and it was a move he claimed he long regretted.

In addition to Newman, Jacqueline Bisset, who shot to stardom after her performance in *Airport* a decade earlier, was hired on as Newman's love interest in the film. William Holden, also from *The Towering Inferno;* Red Buttons and Ernest Borgnine, from *The Poseidon Adventure*; and Veronica Hamel from *Beyond the Poseidon Adventure*, also accepted starring roles. Rounding out the all-star cast was James Franciscus, Barbara Carrera, Alex Karras, Burgess Meredith and Valentina Cortesa.

The story takes place at a luxury resort on a remote tropical island. When the island's long-dormant volcano comes to life again a vast collection of hotel guests are thrown into peril. Similar to the *Poseidon Adventure*, a small band of hotel guests elect to go along with a rugged oil driller, played by Paul Newman, while the remaining guests, believing the volcano will never actually blow, stay behind at the urging of James Franciscus.

The group with Newman, made up of former flame Bisset, hotel owner Holden, elderly couple Meredith and Cortesa, as well as Buttons and a blind Ernest Borgnine, are forced to face the powers of Mother Nature to escape before the final volcano blast that sends lava flooding downhill to destroy the resort and everything else in its path. Allen reportedly spent so much on hiring the all-star cast that, once again, special effects spending was sacrificed to finish the film.

A Dismal Release

The film was released on March 28, 1980 to dismal reviews. *Variety* wrote that Allen had, "once again gathered some heavy box office names, thrown them into seemingly hopeless peril and dared them to get out alive. Given the public's ever-increasing resistance to these kinds of offerings, pic's stay at theaters should be relatively short."

The New York Times was harder on the

film, saying the film was "waxen even by Mr. Allen's standards," while *The Christian Science Monitor* wrote, "The presence of Paul Newman doesn't help, though the presence of Jacqueline Bisset almost helps."

The final budget for the film reportedly topped $22 million, but the film earned a mere $1.7 million at the box office, rating as one of the biggest failures of the year.

Interestingly enough, *When Time Ran Out* had an ironic brush with reality, but the unplanned promotion apparently was too little too late.

The film opened in late March and managed to hang on in theaters through April even with the poor reviews and in mid May, as the film was ending its brief run in movie houses, volcanic eruptions caught headlines around the world when Mt. St. Helens erupted in the Pacific Northwest. It was called the "largest volcanic eruption in historic times on the mainland United States causing widespread damage and taking six lives.

The timing of the event was ironic, but by then the damage was done and *When Time Ran Out* was regarded as a failure and the reality wasn't enough to breathe new life into the picture.

One other quasi-disaster picture was released in 1980 as well and found a similar fate. *Virus* was a $17 million Japanese picture about a deadly germ wreaking havoc on humanity. The mediocre all-star cast in this one featured Glenn Ford, Robert Vaughn, Chuck Conners, Olivia Hussey and George Kennedy, but problems between the Japanese crew and the English-speaking stars made filming difficult and the resulting picture failed at the box office, earning only about $2 million in its release. Time literally had run out on the disaster picture.

thirteen
The Return of the Disaster Film

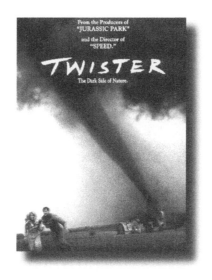

New Life for the Disaster

Roughly 25 years after *Airport* launched the first wave of disaster pictures, the genre had a renaissance in 1996. It was a return to the big screen that rivaled the success of the original wave, setting the stage for bigger pictures, bigger budgets and bigger profits. There were a number of factors that caused the resurgence of the disaster picture, but none more prevalent than the advances in computer technology.

With the advent of the computer age, filmmaking found a new partner. The advances in computer technology in the late 1980s and early 1990s created boundless opportunities for Hollywood as digital effects took over the world of moviemaking. It wasn't so much that digital effects were a novel idea. For years Hollywood had been using digital photography effects to enhance its films. But by the early 1990s the technology was becoming refined and no longer looked as "fake" as it had years before when it was most often merged with actors and live action. Now, it was becoming difficult to tell what was real and what was not and the skill at merging live action with digital effects was becoming far easier and much less expensive that it had just a few years earlier.

Initially, effects were a supporting role in many of the action, adventure and horror films of the late 1980s early 90s. James Cameron's work in *The Terminator* features and *The Abyss* began testing the waters for expanding the use of effects in features. The success of the films showed that moviegoers would pay to be wowed by fantastic visual effects created by computers, just as they had been by effects in features like *Star Wars, Close Encounters of the Third Kind* and *The Towering Inferno* of the 1970s.

Twist and Shout

By the beginning of 1995 two Hollywood studios joined forces to create a film that really centered on the use of computer-generated effects. While other films worked on story, plot or characters alone, with effects thrown in for excitement or climactic scenes, this time the use of effects would make or break the film, for without them there was no movie. The film was *Twister*.

Just as Fox and Warner Bros. had joined together to produce *The Towering Inferno* 20 years earlier, Warner Bros. and Universal agreed to bankroll an estimated $30 million to produce a film. The story centered on tornadoes sweeping through the heartland of America and a band of trackers that follow them, looking for ways to learn from them and possibly one day predict them with enough precision that they can save the lives of people in their path. Warner Bros. was to receive the domestic profits from the release of the film while Universal earned the international box office receipts.

Back when *Airport* was made, $10 million was an expensive picture and the most expensive picture to date had been *Cleopatra* in 1963, which topped out at an estimated $38-40 million. By the mid-90s, $30 million was below the average price for a studio-produced picture

— it was actually closer to $50 million. The marketing and promotion alone was averaging out at nearly $30 million as well, but the promise of high returns for a hit returning $100 million at the box office, tied with video sales, worldwide distribution, and promotional tie-ins made the risk worth taking. And with the summer movie season being responsible for about 40 percent of a year's ticket sales, it became easier to target the best time to take that risk.

For *Twister*, the two studios hired director Jan De Bont to make the film with a release date set for Memorial Day 1996, launching the summer movie season. De Bont was at the helm of *Speed* in 1994, an action adventure film about a bus with a bomb on board. The disaster-like feature was filmed for roughly $30 million, but pulled in some $60 million in the U.S. and an estimated $160 million in its international release.

Creating a Blockbuster

The story for *Twister* was by Michael Crichton and his wife Anne Marie Martin. Crichton was best known for his books-to-

126

movies works like *Jurassic Park, Disclosure* and *The Andromeda Strain*, while Anne Marie Martin originally found success as an actress on the soap opera *Days of Our Lives*.

By January, 1995 Bill Paxton was named one of the stars of the picture and De Bont was searching for the female lead to play opposite him. In February it was announced that Helen Hunt, whose fame had come from her starring role on TV's *Mad About You*, was going to take the role. Hunt accepted the part, passing on another opportunity to star opposite John Travolta in *Broken Arrow*.

By March there was talk that Mira Sorvino was also to star in *Twister*, but in April in was announced that Paxton and Hunt would co-star with Jami Gertz and Cary Elwes, with the production set to begin filming in May.

To make the disaster real, the combination of the filmed feature with computer-generated effects had to be seamless. The actors had to move in tune with effects that would be added in later. And while this had been going on for years, in *Twister* the effects were constant,

not just a few key scenes that it had to be done perfectly in order for the movie to hold together.

Location shooting took the cast and crew to the heartland, with filming taking place in numerous towns in Oklahoma, with additional footage in Iowa and Texas. Film crews actually began showing up in Oklahoma in February, with three units on site studying and chasing tornadoes. Producer Kathleen Kennedy when asked why Oklahoma, replied, "Well, this is a movie about tornadoes, and I think that answers the question."

A film crew of about 175 to 200 people was assembled and the National Severe Storms Laboratory agreed to provide technical assistance. Small towns like Pauls Valley, Wakita, Ponca City, as well as Osage, Kay, Garfield, Pawnee, Noble, McLain and Grant counties in Oklahoma geared up for their time in the spotlight. It was reported that several million dollars from the filming would be pumped into the local economies. Even so, some towns held community meetings discuss their concerns about the impact the filming would have on the local communities as 200 crew members, dozens of extras and the stars of the movie descended on the towns. In fact, many of the extras in the film came from the towns themselves and were paid about $55 a day for 10 hours of work, giving locals their chance at stardom.

Some structures were torn down to show the destruction left by a tornado and the local electric company agreed to take down some power lines and telephone poles to add to the destructive atmosphere. In addition, some building facades were added to towns only to be torn down for after the twister scenes.

Without surprise several twisters reportedly swept through the Oklahoma area during filming, although none hit the production directly. One tornado hit the southern part of the state in early May killing three people and the cast and crew were advised of the safety precautions in the event a real twister came through.

Filming in Oklahoma lasted until early July. Some additional shots of cornfields and other helicopter landscape shots were done in Iowa. One Iowa scene called for a severe storm to hit the area. To achieve the shot a jet engine was placed on a hill with a large debris hopper o top of it and six men shoveling branches leaves and other debris into it that would be blown out, mirroring the effects of a twister. At the same time three large ice chutes on a flatbed took in 40 400-pound blocks of ice, chopping them up and spewing them out before the cameras to produce hail.

Hunt and Paxton recalled that the hail scenes were the worst to shoot. "There were ice machines to crush the ice so thin that it wouldn't be like hitting us with rocks, but the problem wa it had to be large enough to be seen," said Hunt. "There were moments when I thought, 'What am I doing here? Is this what acting is all about?'"

The real weather was almost as unpredictable as the weather in the script with periods of intense rain, then sunshine, then hard winds. De Bont called it, "not only unpredictable, but incredible."

But the weather wasn't the only thing unpredictable. Reports of trouble between the director and his crew created major concerns for the producers. One report said that the creative differences between De Bont and the director of photography Don Burgess resulted in Burgess leaving the production and being replaced. It was reported that Burgess and more than 20 camera people walked off the production at one point, rumored to be after the director called the team "incompetent."

In another troubled moment, the crew became upset after De Bont pushed a camera assistant into the mud after the assistant got in the way of a complicated camera shot. "With the wind machines it was very loud, so the crew had to watch my hand signals," explained De Bont. "I cued action, and he [walked] right in the middle of the scene. We kept losing good performances because of stupid things like that. I don't think I'm a hothead, but I do believe you have to be passionate. These crews get paid well, and when they screw up, I'm going to call them on it."

Star Bill Paxton admitted, "Sure, there are hardships. You don't put a story like this on the screen without paying the freight," while Hunt said making the movie was "a great experience."

Creating the Effects

When location shooting wrapped and the special effects work took over Industrial Light & Magic (ILM) came on board to develop the more than 200 digital shots required for the film. Some of the shots were so complex it was reported that the technology was still being developed to make the scenes work. "It's a whole new world with digital effects," said De Bont during the production. "It will help us change moviemaking."

De Bont was amazed at the quality of the effects, saying "The tests are so photo-realistic, people think it's documentary footage."

ILM created the Midwestern twisters at its special effects factory in San Rafael, California, where it has been located since the last 1970s. ILM has been responsible for effects work on numerous features including *Jurassic Park, Terminator 2* and *The Abyss*. For *Twister*,

ILM used some 150 people to work on the effects and found it one of the most challenging projects.

The film had more than four times as many effects as *Jurassic Park*, taking up some 25 minutes of screen time. In addition, the challenge of creating a tornado that looked and acted real took time and care.

In addition to the twisters, the effects team was required to hurl cars and trucks through the air and create a host of post-tornado after-effects.

The tornadoes themselves were drawn on the computer screens and then mathematical programs were used to generate rough looking surfaces that were combined with actual footage. The colors of the twisters were altered to make them look more ominous and ILM used darker specs to simulate debris, then they used a computer program to make the funnel turn. "Twister couldn't have been made without digital effects," admitted the director.

The Picture is Finished

When it was all said and done, the final budget total in at more than $70 million and an addition marketing budget brought the cost closer to $100 million, but the studios saw a hit and began planning for the release.

Originally set to open Memorial Day Weekend, launching the summer movie season, the studio pushed the opening up, knowing they had a hit on their hands and eager to create a stir at the box office. With so many films competing for attention during summer months the bigger the launch the better. So, *Twister* opened nationwide on May 10th, several weeks early and beating the competition to the movie house. It was the number one movie and both critics and moviegoers were positive about the film. The effects and action created the excitement, however, some critics found the story and characters a little weak.

The San Francisco Examiner called the story "about as dull as a prairie vista," and summed it up as, "Big swirls of computer-generated dirt, a bickering couple ..." As for the special effects the reviewer added "If inclement climactic conditions do it for you, then this is your movie."

The San Diego Union Tribune was more responsive, writing, "*Twister* is not loaded with the old stars who once packed such Irwin Allen disaster epics like *The Poseidon Adventure, The Swarm* and *The Towering Inferno*. But it's a barn-smashing, tree-ripping starter for Movie Summer '96, with credible actors and some fairly credible effects."

For the most part the story was called credible, but predictable, while the special effects were singled out as the most compelling reason to see the film on the big screen. The film took in more than $230 million at the domestic box office making it one of the biggest hits of the year. And after the box office success, a new era in disaster films was dawning.

fourteen
Mixing the Old and the New

Disaster Sees 'Daylight'

Universal gave birth to the modern disaster picture with *Airport* back in 1970. What followed was the subsequent rise and fall and rise again of the disaster picture. After the success of *Twister*, Universal once again stepped back into the creation of the disaster film, hoping to recapture the success of its illustrious past.

It was in 1995 that MCA/Universal was purchased by Seagram Co. and the studio began an aggressive campaign to make "big" movies. To that end it began making deals with major directors and major stars to create big-budget pictures for the studio. And with the disaster film making a comeback the studio saw an opportunity to strike while the iron was hot.

And while it was key that the 1970s disaster picture featured an all-star cast, the 1990s vehicle no longer had that requirement.

Twister proved that special effects created via computer could now be the draw. Dollars once used for stars could be used for effects instead. But what Universal believed, was that big names meant big dollars, but effects would still help sell a movie. Instead of an all-star cast they opted for a single star vehicle that would combine the elements of both the old disaster picture of the 1970s and the newer 90s version. The film was *Daylight*.

A Major Star Vehicle

Universal purchased the original script by Leslie Bohem in October 1994 for $1.2 million. A number of actors had expressed interest in the lead role, but the studio wanted a star with international box office draw and offered the part to Sylvester Stallone.

Stallone signed onto the picture for a reported $17.5 million and inked a three-picture deal with Universal for $60 million. Stallone's deal also included a percentage of the film's box office. It was one of the first of a wave of mega-money deals Universal and other studios were making to compete in the ever-increasing high-stakes world of Hollywood. *Daylight* would take Stallone on somewhat familiar territory, but under different circumstances.

King of Adventure

It was nearly 20 years earlier when Stallone began his journey as king of the action/adventure pictures. *Rocky* was an Oscar-winning tour-de-force for Stallone and the film's success led to a string of sequels as well as a series of other action features that pulled in major box-office dollars, but little critical acclaim. But soon Stallone had competition as Arnold Schwarzenegger and Bruce Willis stepped up to bat as major action stars, but while both Schwarzenegger and Willis also found success in comedy and more romantic features, Stallone was pegged as an action star and any efforts of his outside the genre seemed to fail.

For Stallone, however, this was initially not a problem. His bank ability as a major action star enabled him his pick of projects and the success of those action pictures enabled

him his occasional escape into the world of comedy or drama. But for his work in *Daylight*, Stallone would be given the opportunity to combine elements of drama and action, with his character being a common man put to the test by disastrous circumstances. This portrayal was reportedly what attracted the actor to the film, because his usual character was a larger-than-life hero using guns and violence to save the day.

Stallone called it "a direction I've wanted to go for years, making the so-called action hero no more grand than anyone in the audience. He's just forced to do it."

Making Things Go Boom

Budgeted at roughly $70 million, filming took place at Cinecitta Studios in Italy, where the U.S. dollar bought more than it did in the states Universal pumped money into the local Italian economy and used the services of foreign producers to set budgets which packaged in not only filming costs, but also taxi, hotel and restaurant costs as well. But, for a star of Stallone's magnitude, certain factors were taken into consideration. In addition to the star's hefty salary, Stallone was also given a jet for his own private use during production, as well as the services of two bodyguards.

Directed by Rob Cohen, who had recently finished filming Universal's *Dragonheart*, production began in late September 1995 and it was hoped the film could be ready for theaters by early July, 1996.

In addition to Stallone, an ensemble cast was developed to take on the supporting roles that revolve around the action of Stallone's character. The actors selected for the roles were of noteworthy talent, but could hardly be considered stars. Amy Brenneman of *Casper* and *NYPD Blue*, Stan Shaw of *Fried Green Tomatoes*, Viggo Mortensen of *Crimson Tide*, Claire Bloom of *Crimes and Misdemeanors*, Colin Fox of *On My Own*, Renoly Santiago of *Dangerous Minds*, Karen Young of *Hoffa*, Trina Davis of *Picket Fences* and Sage Stallone, the star's son, who had also starred in *Rocky V*, made up the quasi-all-star cast.

The story initially begins developing the cast of characters, on their way to various destinations, when a freak accident caused by some reckless youths leads to a truck carrying explosive chemicals to crash inside an underwater tunnel connecting New York and New Jersey. When both ends of the tunnel are sealed off by the massive explosion, a handful of survivors are trapped inside, desperate to get out. A former emergency services chief, played by Stallone, manages to find his way into the tunnel, but becomes trapped along with the other survivors and it's up to him to lead the group to safety. Similar to *The Poseidon Adventure* and *The Towering Inferno*, floods, fires, and personality clashes face the small group of survivors, who must work together to survive the ordeal.

For the massive explosion, the producers built a 1/3-mile-long, full-scale tunnel, complete with toll booths at both ends, as well as a miniature, 1/4 the size of the original, and used a combination of live-action and computer animation to create the scene. Industrial Light & Magic was brought on board for the effects work. The initial explosion alone reportedly cost $8 million. Cameras inside the tunnel were housed in fireproof cases and operated by remote control, while the cars that drove into the tunnel were actually pulled by cables and dummies were placed inside the cars so no one would be injured during the explosive sequence. Close-up shots of actors caught inside the fiery tunnel were film separately and edited into the other footage and miniatures were used to show the tunnel caving in, trapping the characters inside. Another major scene was done full scale with the actors in the shot when a 50-foot slab of the ceiling which was designed to crack, break open on cue, sending a flood of muddy water, supposedly the Hudson River, flowing through, drenching the actors. Enormous water tanks and industrial pumps were used to get the scene right.

The structure of the film paid homage to Irwin Allen's feature so closely that many reviewers saws the similarities between the film and *The Poseidon Adventure* and *The Towering Inferno*.

A Worldwide Release

Once the filming and special effects work were completed the film was slated for a December 6th opening, which was behind initial plan, but had special significance. The date had meaning for Stallone because it marked the 20th anniversary of the opening of his first major motion picture, *Rocky*. And while films usually open first in the U.S. and move into worldwide release later, for *Daylight* the studio opted for a global release with the film opening around the world on the same date. The move was an important one because Stallone was not viewed as a major draw in the U.S. at the time, having had several notable failures. Yet, as an international star, the actor continued to prove himself bankable. And if *Daylight* performed poorly during its domestic release, it could reflect on the international release, but if it was released internationally at the same time, a poor U.S. showing would have little effect.

The move proved to be a good one, because the film failed to create much interest during its Christmas release in 1996. Battling against *101 Dalmations* for the holiday box office, *Daylight* pulled in only about $10 million during its first week and by the end of its domestic run the film earned only $35 million. However, internationally the film fared much better, earning as much as $120 million.

Reviews for the film were mostly poor, although far from horrible. Most reviewers felt there was little for the actors to do beyond stunt work in the film and that the effects, which were supposed to be a key draw for the film, were far from fantastic after witnessing the visual work done in *Twister*. Reviewers and audiences probably expected more and were disappointed. *Variety* called it "claustrophobic" and wrote that the film "features plenty of big explosions and close calls, but nothing that will blow audiences away. Technical contributions are elaborate, but tight, dark quarters in which most of the story unfolds give the enterprise a squeezed, somewhat dingy feel."

However, *Daylight* proved to be successful enough after adding in promotional efforts gained from an Internet Web site that included a game based on the feature, as well as video sales and rentals, and the movie soundtrack. Universal was already moving forth with another addition to the growing list of new wave disaster features.

fifteen
The Battle of the Volcanoes Begins

'Dante's Peak' Erupts

With heart-stopping effects now only a keystroke away and the studios having seen the success of *Twister*, as well as *Daylight*, several studios were working on new disaster flicks as the genre found renewed success. If computer generated twisters could wow audiences, other major disasters could do the same and soon. So, just like in the 70s, Hollywood was looking at fire, floods and a host of other natural disasters to create movie magic.

Next up, the volcano was due for an eruption and two scripts came about at roughly the same time. Unlike 20 years earlier, when Irwin Allen convinced two studios making burning skyscraper pictures to join together for one big film, this time the projects were both greenlighted for production and went racing toward the big screen. *Dante's Peak* and *Volcano* were the features, with *Dante's Peak* arriving first.

Dante's Peak

Universal was again out in front with the disaster picture in mid-1996 when it began filming *Dante's Peak*, following up on *Daylight*.

Costing an estimated $115 million, *Dante's Peak* starred Pierce Brosnan as volcanologist Harry Dalton, who arrives at the Pacific Northwest town of Dante's Peak to investigate an increase in seismic activity. He becomes confident that the long dormant volcano beside the sleepy town is about to erupt, but before he can convince the town and his supervisor of his suspicions the volcano does just that, sending everyone running for their lives. Dalton, who has fallen for the town's mayor, Linda Hamilton, takes off with her to rescue her two young children and former mother-in-law who are directly in the volcano's path.

The big-budget effects would use both miniatures and computer animation to destroy the small town, collapsing its buildings, blowing out windows, tossing cars, snapping bridges and covering everything in tons of ash. In addition, a disastrous flow of lava would bring trouble as the major cast members struggle for survival.

Director Roger Donaldson, who was best known for character-driven films like *No Way Out, Cocktail, Cadillac Man* and *Mutiny on the Bounty*, was brought in to direct the picture. Producer Gale Anne Hurd who found success in action adventures like *The Terminator* films, *Aliens* and *The Abyss* came aboard to produce. Together, it was hoped that the duo would combine strong characters and human interest with a rollercoaster ride of adventure.

Universal initially wanted to sign a major leading man to the role in the film for an estimated $20 million, much like it had done with Sylvester Stallone in *Daylight*. Again, the studio possibly felt a star with international draw would ensure success with the big budget feature. The director, however, had other ideas and pushed the studio to let him hire a friend of his, Pierce Brosnan, for the lead role. Brosnan's major claim to fame had come in television with the hit series *Remington Steele* several years

earlier but had now taken over the lead in the James Bond series and was poised for big screen success. However, his appeal at this point was not as worldwide as the studio had hoped, but they agreed to the casting and Brosnan was paid $5 million for his efforts, leaving additional dollars for the special effects.

In August, the film crew descended on the small town of Wallace, Idaho for location filming. The old mining town attracted the director because a nearby canyon gives Wallace a look that it's walled off from the rest of the world. Donaldson and crew changed the town's name to Dante's Peak and cleaned things up a bit for filming, adding flowers and shrubs, as well as building a church and a bank that would be torn down by the explosion. In addition, 300 town locals were cast as extras in the film with the director remarking, "Look at these extras! You couldn't get extras like that in L.A. They look like real people."

The production crew spent two months on location pumping a reported $10 million in the local economy, before heading back to

Hollywood for post-production work.

For the effects, Donaldson built a small version of the town and volcano in an airplane hanger using wood, Styrofoam and stucco. The crew spent two months perfecting a 35-foot volcano that was placed over mortar cannons filled with gravel and ash. Explosive charges were used to set off the explosion and the results were filmed. Following the destruction, 260,000 pounds of shredded newspaper were used as ash to cover everyone and everything on the screen. Computer-generated effects that tore apart the town and were merged with the actual filmed footage to make the disaster look real.

Scripted by Leslie Bohem, who gave moviegoers Stallone's *Daylight*, the feature finished filming in late October and was set for a March 1997 release, hoping to beat *Volcano* to the big screen and reap the success of its early release. It was a bold move for the studio in some regards because the summer box office season was the most logical time for the action adventure, but the stiff competition could prove costly. Producer Hurd said she had no concerns about the competition, seeing both volcano movies as very different and had few worries about the early release date. "They're so different, they're not going to cancel each other out," said Hurd. Hurd also explained, "It's been proven that you can have a successful release any time of the year. Hits like *The Hunt for Red October* were released in March."

The release dates for *Dante's Peak* and *Volcano* were jockeying for position by November when Fox set *Volcano*'s premiere date for February 28, putting it in theaters before *Dante's Peak*, which had a release date of March 7. When Universal pushed up their release to February 7, *Volcano* gave in and moved their release date back to late April, hoping to separate the films and avoid direct competition.

The Reviews Are In

Once again, like most disaster films, *Dante's Peak* earned mediocre reviews. While most applauded the special effects work achieved on the big screen, some said the film lost its steam in the final scenes and that it spent more time on the special effects than it did on the characters. Comparing the film to *Twister,* one reviewer wrote, "Unlike last summer's swirling disaster epic, which contained just enough human interaction and narrative energy to keep it from being merely and amusement park ride, this latest salvo in the cinema of natural destruction is virtually devoid of believable human activity."

But not all the reviews centered on the troubles of *Dante's Peak.* Focusing on the strengths, another reviewer wrote, "*Dante's Peak* does one thing right: it dazzles us with special effects. Where the 70s disaster films played on our sympathy for its terror-stricken characters (and usually did it poorly), *Dante's Peak* focuses on the sheer power of the erupting volcano. The 70's films tried to build characters that we'd care about, failing to understand that we didn't care about a whiny Shelley Winters stuck on a sinking ship (we just wished Shelley, the ship and the film would sink already)."

In the end the movie fared well at the box office, taking in $18.5 million in its opening weekend alone and pulling in $67 million in its domestic box office release and topping $100 million internationally. And with video rentals, sales and other merchandising the filmed proved to be somewhat successful for Universal.

It had beaten *Volcano* the big screen, but the question on everyone's mind was would it beat the film in quality, effects, and most importantly, in box office returns. A few months later, Hollywood had its answer.

sixteen
Eruption of a New Volcano

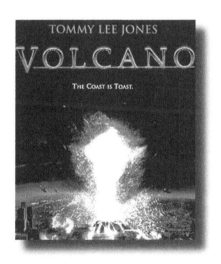

Fox Unveils Its Volcano

Once *Dante's Peak* set its release
date for early February 1997, the producers of
Volcano settled into their position as the second
volcano picture of the year and looked forward
to their release in April. It was a risk, but by that
point there was little they could do to change
things.

Facing the Competition

Releasing *Volcano* in April held promise
by kicking off the summer movie season early
with a big opening. *Twister* had shown an
early season opening could succeed and it's
probable that the makers of *Volcano* hoped that
lightning would strike twice. Not only does the
early opening beat other summer pictures to the
movie house, limiting tough competition, but the
option also allows films a chance at a longer run

in theaters. If initial success convinces movie
houses to hold the picture because if ticket sales
are strong, box office returns can be tremendous,
which was the case for *Twister*.

On the down side, however, some
predicted that the earlier release of *Dante's Peak*
would steal *Volcano*'s thunder. And when *Peak*
found mixed reviews and only a so-so box office,
Volcano's producer had reason to worry about
whether their film would be seen by moviegoers
as just another *Dante's Peak* and stay away from
the theater. As film editor for the *Hollywood
Reporter*, Stephen Galloway, told *The New York
Post*, "Clearly, each one undermined the other.
Audiences go see these pictures to see what the
effects look like — and when they've already
seen it, they don't bother going again.
And, if the competition of *Dante's Peak* wasn't
enough, *Volcano* had television to contend with
as well. February rating sweeps found NBC
taking to the airways with a two-part miniseries
call *Asteroid*, which used similar visual effects
to draw its audience. While the miniseries was
panned by critics, it came out on top in the

ratings and possibly gave moviegoers one less reason to head to the theater to see *Volcano*.

Whatever the case, Fox's *Volcano* took in only $14.7 million in its opening weekend, compared to *Peak*'s more than $18 million, which spelled trouble for the long-term release. When it was said and done *Volcano* earned only $47.5 million in its domestic release, while *Peak* took in more than $67 million. Internationally, the film took in somewhere in the neighborhood of $60 million, so the total box office barely covered the estimated $95 million it cost to produce and the film. Only subsequent video rentals and sales would help the film show a profit.

The Story

Unlike *Dante's Peak*, *Volcano*'s path of destruction didn't take place in a remote little town near a sleeping volcano. The drama in the *Volcano* takes place in Los Angeles, giving the promotion of the film a catch tagline — "The Coast is Toast."

The story for the film takes off when a large earthquake opens a crack beneath the surface of the earth, allowing molten lava deep inside the earth to climb to the surface, bubbling up in the La Brea Tar Pits. Soon the lava is flowing through the city's subway tunnels and streets, destroying everything and everyone in its path.

For the leading man, Fox originally offered the role to Bill Pullman who had succeeded recently with *Independence Day*. But Pullman wanted $7 million for the role and was hesitant about taking another major special effects project. The studio only offered him $5 million and when he asked for more Fox turned to Tommy Lee Jones, who earned an Oscar for his performance in the blockbuster *The Fugitive*. Jones took on the lead role of the director of L.A.'s emergency services office who is a single father with a troubled teenager, played by Gaby Hoffman. Anne Heche took the leading actress role in the film, portraying a seismologist who figures out what's happening and helps Jones find a solution to the problem and save as much of the city as they can.

Screenwriter Jerome Armstong reportedly

came up with the idea for the film with the help of a few strangers. "About two years ago [1995] I was standing on a street corner in Santa Monica and I overheard two people talking. One guy said to the other, 'We've had earthquakes, fires, floods, mudslides — what could possibly happen to us next?'"

Six months later Armstrong had apparently come up with the answer and sold his idea to Fox Filmed Entertainment. It wasn't until after the deal was sealed that Fox learned of Universal's competing volcano picture.

Fox reportedly went to Universal and suggested combining the two features, but the two studios couldn't reach an agreement on the combined feature, so both pictures began the race to the big screen.

The Critics Are Back

Critics called the film preposterous and 'so implausible-it's almost believable," but again, special effects carried the film with scenes of molten lava flowing through the streets of Los Angeles. But effects were not enough to draw moviegoers. To capture the destruction, the producers built a replica of five square blocks of downtown Los Angeles inside an airplane hanger, which they then destroyed.

For the key role of the lava, the special effects team needed something that was "really thick and goocy, but at the same time not environmentally horrific."

What they found was an ingredient called methylcellulose, which is most commonly used for thickening milkshakes at fast food restaurants. They mixed the stuff with fluorescent colors to make the lava glow.

For the actors, the problem was reacting to special effects that weren't even there. It's a common problem for most science fiction and disaster films. But since the lava was a major character in the film, it was a serious issue to deal with for several key scenes and concerned some cast members. "You don't want to mess up on a big action movie where there're 50,000 extras running around," said Anne Heche in an interview. "You wouldn't want to be the person to stop everything because you forgot your line."

And while some might have thought that

Hollywood would begin to question the future of

the making of big budget disaster pictures again,

the reality was quite the opposite.

seventeen
Taking the Disaster to a Whole New Level

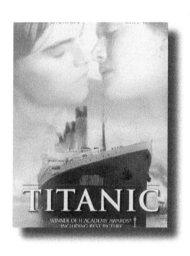

Titanic Makes Movie History

The disaster picture reached a new milestone in 1998 when *Titanic* took home Academy Awards for Best Picture and Best Director, along with a host of other honors for special effects, costumes and more. And when the film took in more than $600 million in its domestic box office release it became the most successful motion picture ever. It also took in more than $1 billion in its worldwide release and millions more when it hit video stores later that year. The merchandising and interest surrounding James Cameron's epic helped make 1997 one of the most memorable and financially rewarding years for Hollywood. But *Titanic* was memorable long before it ever hit the big screen.

The sinking of the actual ocean liner on its maiden voyage in 1912 has long been the subject of interest and fascination. Promoted as unsinkable, the Titanic took the lives of some 1,500 passengers when it hit an iceberg in the North Atlantic in April, 1912. Only about 700 of the 2,200 passengers were able to escape because there were too few lifeboats aboard the ship that fateful evening. The loss of life and shock of the unthinkable happening became legendary.

In 1953, Barbara Stanwyck, Clifton Webb and Robert Wagner starred in *Titanic,* and in 1958 a British film called *A Night to Remember* also told the story of the fateful ocean liner. Special effects used miniatures to capture the actual sinking and the stories were told using a select group of passengers, some fictional and some real, to bring the disaster to a human level. The 1997 remake would follow the same path, but because of advances in digital technology, Cameron could utilize new technology to bring the ship back to life for another tragic collision with an iceberg.

Creating an Epic

Filmmaker James Cameron was known for making the impossible possible. His features had been pushing the envelope of special effects for some time. And while the cost of his films was usually high, the resulting box office success made him one of the most bankable directors in Hollywood. Hits like *Terminator, Aliens, The Abyss* and *True Lies* reaped $1.2 billion at the box office, so when the director decided *Titanic* would be his next effort, Hollywood was preparing for something spectacular.

Cameron reportedly started working on the script for the film back in 1992. The project kicked into high gear in the September, 1995 when the director used two remote-controlled video cameras he helped develop to travel 2.5 miles beneath the surface of the ocean to film the wreckage of the real Titanic. The remarkable footage from the cameras was unveiled in early October during a marine technology convention when Cameron announced plans for the movie and to use the footage in the final film. The director called the filming experience "very eerie" and said, "When we were done, I threw a wreath in the water. It just seemed like the respectful thing to do."

Titanic, he hoped, would pay respect to those who lost their lives on the ship and would educate the world, offering the latest information about what really happened. For years speculation and rumor surrounding the sinking had experts theorizing on what course of events caused the unsinkable ship to sink.

Paramount and Twentieth Century Fox announced a joint effort to produce the film with Paramount handling the U.S. release and Fox distributing the film abroad. The film was initially budgeted at $110 million making it the most expensive disaster picture to date.

Casting the Stars

Casting on the picture began in early 1996, and again, like many disaster pictures of the past, an ensemble cast of notable actors would be assembled for the feature. Leonardo DiCaprio, who earned an Oscar nomination for *What's Eating Gilbert Grape* and starred in a big screen remake of *Romeo and Juliet,* was announced as the leading man by early March. Kate Winslet was shortly after signed on as leading lady. Winslet, who was nominated for an

Oscar for her role in *Sense and Sensibility,* would play a wealthy young woman aboard the ship who falls for DiCaprio, a poor artist traveling in steerage.   In addition, Kathy Bates, Oscar winner for her role in *Misery*, accepted the part of Molly Brown, while Frances Fisher would portray Winslet's mother and Billy Zane would be Winslet's fiancé. Bill Paxton and Gloria Stewart took roles in the present day with Stewart playing Kate Winslet's character and Paxton as a bounty hunter who brings Stewart back out to sea looking for treasure in the ship's wreckage.

An Exhausting Production

The production was as huge as the original ship itself and the troubles behind the disaster were nearly as great. The days were long and exhausting, according to cast and crew and Cameron's determination for perfection had some wondering if the picture would ever really be finished. "The first day started at 5 a.m. and went on to 1 a.m.," recalled Winslet. "Nothing could have prepared me for it. There were quite a few 20-hour days. And two-thirds of it was night shooting — because the Titanic sunk at night. It was every man for himself on the set — you had to ensure that you snatched some sleep during the day, with a black eye mask on. Sometimes you'd find yourself having lunch at 2 a.m. or breakfast at 4 p.m. It was very disorienting."

Cameron's obsessive nature was well known throughout Hollywood, but not something he'd apologize for. "Filmmaking is so all-consuming that if you're not spending 24-hours a day at it, you're slipping off your game," admitted the director. "Being obsessive is true of any good filmmaker. I personally don't know any directors who are any good whatsoever if they're not obsessive about their work."

To film the epic, Cameron built a 700-foot replica of the Titanic — the real ship was 882 feet — but Cameron's only had one side looking like the real thing for filming. The ship was built in a large tank, which was then filled with water. The water was heated to 72 degrees to keep the actors from getting too cold.

In addition to the ship, Cameron had a new studio built in Mexico to house the cast and crew because no location set was large enough to handle the job. Other location shooting took place in Los Angeles, Nova Scotia and Britain.

Location shooting in Rosario Beach, Mexico took roughly six months with a variety of mishaps and problems. Winslet reportedly chipped a small bone in her elbow in one scene, nearly drowned twice and suffered hypothermia after lengthy time in the water. Some reports claimed the film crew was putting in 80-hour, six-day work weeks, with some crew working as much as two weeks straight without breaks. "I think it's the closest thing to slavery that I've ever laid my eyes on," Elizabeth Bolden, a set rigger who spent a month on the Mexico set, told *Time* magazine.

While others have denied the allegations, some crew reported working as long as 10 hours without a break and some reports had local crew members receiving only bread and water during endless 12-hour days.

In August, 1996, nearly 80 members of the cast and crew, including Bill Paxton and James Cameron, suffered "toxic poisoning" after it was reported that two unknown food workers on the Halifax set spiked the lobster chowder with PCP or angel dust. The crew began vomiting and hallucinating and many were hospitalized. Food poisoning was initially suspected, but lab tests revealed the drug had been placed in the food. Food service officials denied their involvement in the drugging and said someone from Hollywood must have done it.

The massive production dragged on, with more troubles, including as many as nine filming-related accidents being reported. However, considering the crew was made up of roughly 800 people, as well as 30 lifeguards, 80 electricians, and 100 stunt people, the problems could not be considered excessive.

Many on the set admitted their admiration for Cameron and his obsessive focus on the film, however, others were put off by what was called his "abrasive, frequent angry outbursts and intolerance of imperfection ..."

"If anything was the slightest bit wrong, he would lose it," said star Kate Winslet. "It was hard to concentrate when he was losing it, shouting and screaming. Logistically, it was a very tough film, for him as much as anyone. By the end I was existing on four hours sleep a day, but Jim was existing on three."

Time for the Effects

When location filming finally came to a close it was time for the extensive special effects work to take over. Initially, it was hoped that the effects work would be finished around April 1997, but when it became apparent that the need for additional work would prolong the project, rumors began traveling about Hollywood that the film would be delayed from its summer 1997 release.

Both Fox and Paramount were concerned about the delays, however, Cameron's vision for the film required his own digital production studio, as well as several other competing digital effects studios to take up work on the film. While the main work revolved around the sinking scenes and was handled by Cameron's Digital Domain, other visual effects work was farmed out to other companies, including Industrial Light & Magic.

Sound effects and musical score work was also progressing, but finally, the decision was made to push back the initial release date from July 2 to a proposed date of July 25. A short time later it was realized that that date was also unlikely and the release date was moved back to November. Eventually, a December 19, 1997 date was set for the film's premiere in the U.S., although some earlier international premieres were held.

The film was a surefire hit. Reviewers applauded Cameron's film for its cinematography and visual effects. The musical score and direction were also cited for making the film work and audiences began lining up to see the film. Some critics were harder on the film than others.

Some cited the performances and story to be the weakest part of the feature, but most urged moviegoers to see the film on the big screen to capture the full effect of its visual impact.

In the end, *Titanic* cost $200 million for production alone and more than $25 million in marketing, making it the most expensive picture ever. But the publicity surrounding the immense expense and the visual accomplishments of Cameron drew moviegoers to the theater to see what all the talk was about. In addition, the matinee idol status of Leonardo DiCaprio drew many young girls to repeat viewings of the feature and soon the film was breaking every box office record in Hollywood.

As a disaster film, *Titanic* utilized all the elements that make the genre work. Talented, well-known actors with star appeal, use of drama, suspense and adventure, a climactic finale and over-the-top special effects drew the public in and created an epic movie going experience that became an event. It brought the disaster film to a new level.

eighteen
Attack of the Asteroids and Meteors

Dueling Disasters

In January 1997 Dreamworks SKG, the studio formed by the immeasurable talents of Steven Spielberg, Jeffrey Katzenberg and David Geffen, announced it was about to begin a project called *Deep Impact*, which would be a remake, of sorts, of the 1951 sci-fi classic *When Worlds Collide*. *When World's Collide*, in fact, was based on a book by Arthur C. Clarke called *The Hammer of God* and tells the story of a comet with Earth directly in it's path and how the people deal with the drama.

The film was not without competition. Hollywood was about to launch *Dante's Peak* and *Volcano* in theaters and the media was already listing the comparisons. TV was also joining in on the revived disaster craze. After having offered its own version of *Earthquake* and *Titanic*, network television launched its own space-age disaster with the four-hour miniseries, *Asteroid*, a $19 million spectacular that pulled in the ratings as computer graphics put earth on a collision course with a series of destructive meteors.

Nevertheless, *Deep Impact* found its way into production in April 1997 with Mimi Leder hired on as director. Leder had most recently wrapped up directing duties on Dreamworks' *The Peacemaker* and was one of the few women directors in Hollywood making an impact on the action/adventure film. Leder's career took off several years earlier in television with Emmy-award winning work on *ER*, as well as acclaimed work on *LA Law* and *China Beach*.

And even after the seeing double trouble surrounding *Dante's Peak* and *Volcano*, *Deep Impact* barely began production when in May, 1997 another meteor disaster picture, *Armageddon*, went before the cameras, hoping there'd be room enough for two meteor disasters in movie theaters in 1998. While Paramount joined forces with Dreamworks to produce and distribute *Deep Impact*, it was Fox and Disney's

Touchstone that were financing *Armageddon*.

In any event, *Deep Impact* was written by Michael Tolkin and Bruce Joel Rubin and was called a "contemporary action thriller that follows three characters through the chaos that ensues when a group of scientists discover that a comet is on a deadly collision course with Earth."

Deep Impact

The producers of *Deep Impact* were, in fact, old friends. Steven Spielberg was joined by David Brown and Richard Zanuck to produce the picture and it was more that 20 years earlier that the three first joined forces for Spielberg's first feature film *The Sugarland Express* and then for his box office smash *Jaws*. In fact, the three men announced their intentions for doing the film back in 1994, but it would take nearly three years before things fell into place. "I am very happy to be working with David and Richard again," said Spielberg at the time. "It took 20 years, but here we are ... beginning a movie that we hope will be a great rollercoaster ride for audiences all over the world."

A cast of stars was announced for the film with Robert Duvall, Tea Leoni, Morgan Freeman, Elija Wood, Vanessa Redgrave, Maximilian Schell and Lee Sobieski taking the leading roles. The film chronicles the lives of several individuals after the world learns of an impending collision with a comet. Because nothing can be done to stop the collision a series of caves are devised to house 20,000 scientists and dignitaries and 180,000 randomly-selected Americans so some people will survive the blast. How the people react to the situation is the basis for the story, while special effects promised to add excitement to the film.

Leder described the film as "more than a standard disaster flick," explaining, "It's more in the *On The Beach* mode, with characters deciding what to do with their lives when they know they only have so long to live."

Location shooting took place in various locales including Washington, D.C. where some 2,100 extras and 1,700 vehicles were used to film a short scene along the Virginia shore where vacationers are cramming the freeways to escape the doom of a monstrous tidal wave which is on its way.

Of course, creating the special effects presented the biggest challenge to disaster moviemakers today and *Deep Impact* was no exception. Similar to *Independence Day*, scenes of exploding cities were computer generated as were massive tidal waves, and while all required considerable time and detail to be created the desired realism, the disastrous comet required specific detail, since it, in many ways, was the actual star of the film.

Scientists describe a comet as "basically a dirty snowball streaking through space." But as the comet nears the sun the melting snow turns into a cloud of gaseous material called a coma, which surrounds the comet creates the tail behind it.

To design a lifelike comet, the effects crew used a strong and translucent fiberglass material for the actual comet and used lighting beneath it to create an icy look. High-pressure carbon dioxide and oxygen were piped through the comet to the surface to create the gaseous

cloud and pellets made of vermiculite — the same material that appears as small white pellets in most potting soil — simulated chunks of ice and snow coming off the surface of the comet.

The film wrapped and the effects were added in time to set a release date in advance of *Armageddon*. Kicking off the summer box office season with an April premiere the producers hoped the $80 million dollar picture would have a strong early showing drawing movie fans and earning big profits as had *Twister* several summers earlier.

A Boost to the Opening

The release date could not have been better set when real life offered a barrage of free publicity. In mid-March scientists announced they had discovered Asteroid 1997 XF11, a one-mile wide asteroid that was calculated as coming within 30,000 miles of earth and possibly colliding with the planet in the year 2028. Trailers for *Deep Impact* were already playing in theaters nationwide and the eerie realism promised to add momentum to the picture's growing hype.

The news media also took advantage of the coincidence, as well, even after it was later announced that the real asteroid would not come closer than 600,000 miles of Earth, posing no threat to mankind. But, because of the two films in production and the real life close call, many began wondering what might really happen in the event a comet or meteor came crashing down on the planet. It was exactly what the producers were hoping for.

The producers of *Deep Impact* reportedly raced their way through production to get their film in theaters before *Armageddon* and intentionally added additional space shots and effects to compete with the action picture. However, the comet for the film was described as the size of Manhattan, while for *Armageddon* the comet was roughly the size of Texas.

Deep Impact opened nationwide on May 8 in more than 3,000 movie houses and broke *Twister*'s debut record in a non-summer weekend earning some $41.2 million dollars. But like most disaster movies the film suffered from mixed reviews. Some called it boring, while others said the film's effects were well worth the big screen viewing. One review applauded the film, calling it "an emotional rollercoaster ride that not only touches your soul, but, surprisingly, entertains you with its well-rounded story, believeable characters and awesome effects."

Another reviewer felt the personal stories "were not all that gripping," but that the filmmakers managed the actions and effects "rather quite well."

Moviegoers continued to turn out to see the picture helping the movie take in some $140 million at the box office before moving onto the world market. Success on the international distribution, as well as video sales and rentals and a $25 million dollar deal with CBS for the television rights, promised the film would well exceed $200 million. Less than two months later it was *Armageddon's* chance to shine.

nineteen

Another Attack from Space

Making an Impact

the success of *Deep Impact* would be a factor in the release of *Armageddon*, the studios proved that there was room for two comet disasters on the big screen.

It was impossible to mention *Deep Impact* without referring to its competitor *Armageddon*. Released within weeks of each other the striking similarities between the two films had all of Hollywood wondering how the success or failure of *Deep Impact* would impact the release of *Armageddon*.

In fact, it was little more than a year earlier when the release of *Dante's Peak* took the wind from *Volcano*'s sail when it arrived in theaters a short time later. But even so, the rivalry between the two studios making the pictures put the films on a collision course with each other and it looked as if a repeat was about to recur.

With *Deep Impact* performing well in theaters the producers of *Armageddon* probably feared the worst. And while it was logical that

Armageddon

It was in January 1997 that Touchstone Pictures, an arm of Disney, announced that Michael Bay would step in to direct the picture, which was to go before the cameras in May, a few weeks behind *Deep Impact's* production start. Written by Jonathan Hensleigh, who also wrote another quasi-disaster story, *Virus*, the feature would be produced by Gale Anne Hurd. Hurd was also the producer of *Dante's Peak* for Universal, which was just about to debut in theaters at the time. This time, the story surrounded another comet headed directly for Earth. The story follows a band of oil drillers who meet up with the comet on its way and plan to drill deep into it and plant explosives, hoping to blow the comet up and save the world from destruction.

The story begins with a meteor shower that destroys the space shuttle and next a series of small meteors come crashing to earth, knocking down the Crysler Building and wreaking havoc on New York City. NASA soon realizes worse things are headed their way and launch a plan of attack. With 18 days to impact, and needing the best driller to drill a hole into the core of the comet so they can blast the thing to bits, NASA recruits Bruce Willis and his drill team and trains them for their flight into space. The action takes off as the team arrives at the comet and plots to save the day.

Bruce Willis, who was making $20 million per picture, was hired as the star of the picture, but unlike several years earlier with Sylvester Stallone's *Daylight, Armageddon's* producers wanted some other name talent co-starring with Willis. Other stars cast in the picture included Ben Affleck, who was finding fame with *Good Will Hunting*; and Billy Bob Thornton of *Slingblade*. Lyv Tyler, Will Patton, Steve Buscemi and several other name actors took supporting roles in the feature.

The filmmakers reportedly needed a great deal of access to NASA in order to make the story work, so a number of high-level phone calls and discussion with NASA official took place. "We basically asked them to open up their front door and let us walk right in," claimed Director Michael Bay.

NASA agreed, although they did require script approval, but the director said they didn't really change anything anyway. The access to NASA proved to be instrumental and the film crew even got access to what NASA called "the White Room," which is a germ-free security clearance area where the astronauts are before they head onto the space shuttle.

Competition

In addition to the worries of *Deep Impact's* impact on the release the studio also faced competition from *Godzilla*, one of the summer's other big action hopefuls, which hit the big screen over Memorial Day weekend. *Godzilla*, however, didn't meet the blockbuster expectations when it hit the big screen and earned poor reviews and a lack of interest from moviegoers. This presented *Armageddon*'s team a good side and a bad. The good news was the competition would be reduced since *Godzilla's* pull was all but gone by the time *Armageddon* was to hit theaters, but the bad news was the public's lack of interest could spell similar doom for *Armageddon*.

Deep *Impact's* impressive debut was still fresh in the collective mind of Hollywood as Touchstone prepared for the July 1st release of *Armageddon*. Boosting hopes was the real life comet discovery that *Deep Impact* had also used to its advantage. The real life discovery was still current and trailers promoting *Armageddon* highlighted the news. Executive producer of the picture, Jerry Bruckheimer joked "We tried to plan it a little closer to the movie's opening, but someone leaked it out."

Some promotional spots for the film were customized to take advantage of the real news reports because, as Bruckheimer saw it, "This makes the picture more real. What you think is fantasy actually could be reality."

The Release

Armageddon reportedly topped out at about $140 million to produce, which put the film in a costlier category than *Deep Impact*, but the promise of greater special effects was expected to draw the action/adventure crowd that may have felt disappointed with *Deep Impact*. And while some have said the success of *Deep Impact* certainly had an effect on the box office draw of *Armageddon*, the picture succeeded despite dire predictions.

While the reviews were again mixed at best, the effects were applauded by many as the main reason to see the picture. Even so, the continued onslaught of action pictures with major explosions and massive destruction was beginning to wear on reviewers and some cited the style and look of the effects were growing common, although *Armageddon* had pumped up the destruction and even the sound.

When all was said and done, *Armageddon* pulled in more than $201 million in its domestic release and went onto further

profits on international screens and video sales
and rentals. It also beat *Deep Impact* on the
television market when ABC plunked down
$35 million for the rights to show the feature on
television, beating *Deep Impact's* TV sale price
by some $10 million.

twenty

And the Disaster Goes On

Conclusion

As evidenced by the success of the disaster films that have graced Hollywood's big screen over the years, the movie-going public always has an appetite for tragedy and disaster. Because the films enable viewers to take part in a tragedy from the comfort of a movie theater, or their living room, the films offer an experience without real death, danger and destruction. And in today's technologically advanced world of moviemaking, the more real the experience, the more we as viewers want to experience it.

Since the success of *Titanic*, and other disasters of the 1990s, the disaster picture has continued to land on the big screen. *The Day After Tomorrow* in 2004 pulled in millions as moviegoers watched the destruction of humanity and mega millions were made on the worldwide release and merchandising of Steven Spielberg's remake of *War of the Worlds* starring Tom Cruise in 2005. The film again helped capture the imagination of Hollywood's past by remaking the 1950s sci-fi classic. But with major stars and massive computer-generated special effects it made the disasters look real.

A new big screen remake called *Poseidon* in 2006 earned millions as a host of new special effects breathed life into Irwin Allen's classic disaster feature. Directed by Wolfgang Peterson, the film cost an estimated $160,000 and made back its cost in the first month of its U.S. release. It was prequeled by a TV movie remake of *The Poseidon Adventure* that gave television viewers another new look at the classic tale of survival with a different set of characters on the ill-fated cruise ship.

Other TV remakes of similar tales, like a TV version of *Titanic* and Airport-like disaster in the air TV movies like *Mayday* and *Deadly Skies* drew viewers and the TV films could achieve much more visually because computer generation eliminated the need for expensive sets and costly

175

productions.

Jodie Foster also brought the airline disaster back to the big screen in the fall of 2005 with her hit *Flightplan*. While more of a drama than a full-fledged disaster, many elements of previous airline features helped keep the story rolling and filmgoers ongoing fascination with trouble in the sky helped the film come out top at the box office. And other big screen remakes of *King Kong* and *Poseidon* show that Hollywood will continue to look to its past for new ideas.

Billions of dollars have been earned on the success of the disaster movie and as technology advances moviemakers will continue to try to find new ways to bring reality of the disaster closer to audiences and find novel ways to get people to plunk down their dollars to see it on the movie screen.

bibliography
Selected Sources and Reference Material

Books

Barker, Clive. *Clive Barker's A-Z of Horror.* 1997. New York. HarperCollins Publishers.

Brode, Douglas. *Lost Films of the Fifties.* 1991. New York. Carol Publishing Group.

Castle, William. *Step Right Up - I'm Gonna Scare the Pants off America.* 1976. New York. Pharos Books.

Diorio, Al. *Barbara Stanwyck.* 1983. New York. Coward-McCann Inc.

Eames, John Douglas. *The MGM Story.* 1990. New York. Portland House.

Finler, Joel W. *The Hollywood Story.* 1988. New York. Crown Publishers, Inc.

Kapsis, Robert E. 1992. *Hitchcock: The Making of a Reputation.* Chicago. The University of Chicago Press.

McCarty, John. *The Fearmakers.* 1994. New York. St. Martin's Press.

McCarty, John. *The Modern Horror Film.* 1990. New York. Carol Publishing Group.

Smith, Ella. *Starring Miss Barbara Stanwyck.* 1974. New York. Crown Publishers Inc.

Spoto, Donald. T*he Art of Alfred Hitchcock.* 1992. New York. Anchor Books.

Magazines, Newspapers and Transcripts

Allen, Henry. "The Biggest Star: Filming 'Airport '79 Concorde' at Dulles. The Washington Post. November 28, 1978.

Allen, Mary. "Stars on Way to South County." The Capital. June 15, 1997.

Allsop, David. "Downhill All the Way." Sunday Times. January 23, 1994.

Anderson, John. "A First Blast of Summer." Newsday. May 10, 1996.
Andrews, Nigel. "Thrills and Spills." Financial Times. March 17, 1984.

Ansen, David. "Help, Help, The Sky is Falling." Newsweek. November 5, 1979.

Ansen, David. "Stormy Weather in Pago Pago." Newsweek. April 23, 1979.

Ansen, David. "On the Poseidon Upside Down." Newsweek. June 11, 1979.

Ansen, David. "On the Poseidon Upside Down." Newsweek. June 11, 1979.

Appelo, Tim. "'Dante's Peak' Puts Town on Map – Then Wipes it Off." Los Angeles Times. August 1, 1996.

Arnold, Gary. "Summer Releases Wait in the Wings." The Washington Post. June 8, 1977.

Arnold, Gary. "'Rollercoaster': A Good Ride For the Amusement Parks." The Washington Post. June 10, 1977.

Arnold, Gary. "Film Notes." The Washington Post. February 27, 1980.

Arnold, Gary. "Fly By Night; The Plumeting $17 Million 'Meteor'." The Washington Post. October 20, 1979.

Arnold, Gary. "Watching the Oscars" The Washington Post. March 29, 1981.

Arnold, Gary. "Film Notes." The Washington Post. May 31, 1978.

Arnold, Gary. "'Hurricane' Blown Away." The Washington Post. April 12, 1979.

Arnold, Gary. "Movies: The Best and the Worst of the 70s." The Washington Post. December 2, 1979.

Arnold, Gary. "Burying Art Alive in Avalanche'." The Washington Post. September 23, 1978.

Arnold, Gary. "Film Notes." The Washington Post. September 20, 1978.

Arnold, Gary. "Summer Offerings." The Washington Post. August 1, 1979.

Arnold, Gary. "Tottering on the Brink of Disaster." The Washington Post. April 1, 1980.

Avasthi, Su. "'Titanic' Gets Second Wind." The New York Times. August 24, 1998.

Avasthi, Su. "Box-Office Collision Course." The New York Post. April 30, 1998.

Avasthi, Su. "Summer's Sizzlers and Fizzlers." The New York Post. August 11, 1998.

Avasthi, Su. "Box-Office Collision Course." The New York Post. April 30, 1998.

Baker, James. "The Sting." Newsweek. August 14, 1978.

Beck, Marilyn and Smith, Stacy Jenel. "Sly's 'Daylight' Set to Blanket the World in One Shot." The Orange County Register. October 31, 1996.

Beck, Marilyn. "Will 'Titanic' Costs Sink Movie?" Tribune Media Services. April 15, 1997.

Beckerman, Jim. "Actor At Work." The Record. October 1, 1997.

Bigelow, Bruce. "New Video Shots Inside Titanic Intrigue Scientists." The San Diego Union-Tribune. October 12, 1995.

Birkhoff, Ruth. " 'Meteor' Junket to a Crater." The Washington Post. October 21, 1979.

Boyar, Jay. "'Peak' – A Stud, a Thud and, Finally, A Dud." The Orlando Sentinel. February 7, 1997.

Braun, Liz. "New Peak in Disaster Spectacle." The Toronto Sun. February 7, 1997.

Brennan, Judy and Watson, Bret. "Funnel Vision." Entertainment Weekly. November 17, 1995.

Browne, Malcolm W. "Asteroid Is Expected to Make a Pass Close to Earth in 2028." The New York Times. March 12, 1998.

Brownfield, Paul. "Action, Comedy, Rarely Taken Seriously by Academy." Variety. January 5, 1998.

Busch, Anita. "With F/X Forcing Delay, 'Titanic's' ETA Still in Play." Variety. April 28, 1997.

Busch, Anita. "Bay Set for 'Armageddon'." Daily Variety. January 10, 1997.

Busch, Anita. "Happy Hour for Deals at Seagram's Studio." Variety. August 19, 1996.

Butler, Robert. "Take Note." The Kansas City Star. August 30, 1996.

Cameron, James. "'Titanic' is a Tough Shoot; What Else is New." Los Angeles Times. May 5, 1997.

Camp, Todd. "Funnel Crowds." The Fort Worth Star-Telegram. May 1, 1996.

Camp, Todd. "Sneak Previews." The Fort Worth Star-Telegram. March 18, 1996.

Carr, Jay. "Human Lives Make 'Deep Impact'." The Boston Globe. May 9, 1998.

Dawtrey, Adam. "A Single-Malt Man for All Film Seasons." Variety. December 2, 1996.

Cels, Roger. "Challengers Left Looking Up As Paramount Goes 'Deep'." The Hollywood Reporter. May 12, 1998.

Champlin, Charles. "Michael Caine Outclasses the Class System." Los Angeles Times. December 31, 1992.

Cox, Dan. "Wood to Make 'Impact' for Paramount." Daily Variety. March 20, 1997.

Cross, Howard. "Dante's Peak." Chattanooga Free Press. February 10, 1997.

Daly, Steve. "Don't Believe Your Eyes." Entertainment Weekly. June 16, 1995.

Davidson, Keay. "Building A Better Tornado in Marin." The San Francisco Examiner. May 9, 1996.

Davis, Sandi. "When Winds Come Sweeping Up the Plain Mock Drive-In Faces Brunt of Film 'Twister'." The Daily Oklahoman. August 25, 1995.

Davis, Sandi. "'Twister' To Premiere At City Hall." The Saturday Oklahoman. March 2, 1996.

Davis, Sandi. "Right Up Their Alley Movie Producers Rely on Severe Storm Lab for Disaster Film's Technical Twists." The Daily Oklahoman. May 3, 1996.

D'Aurizio, Elaine. "Film Thriller Has N.J. Origin." The Record. November 17, 1996.

Della Cava, Marco R. " 'Apollo 13' Star Plunges Into 'Twister'." USA Today. July 7, 1995.

Denerstein, Robert. "'Twister' Spins Predictable Plot. Rocky Mountain News. May 10, 1996.

Desowitz, Bill. "Sound Stages." Los Angeles Times. July 6, 1997.

Diggs, Mitchell. "Everything You Wanted to Know About Jaws But Were Afraid to Ask." Pittsburgh-Post Gazette. July 30, 1995.

Dreher, Rod. "For 'Impact' Studios, The Earth Moved." The New York Post. May 12, 1998.

Ebert, Roger. "'Dante's Peak' Offers Tired Disaster Film Formula With New Premise." Universal Press Syndicate. February 7, 1997.

Eder, Richard. "Screen: Poisonous 'Bug.' The New York Times. September 18, 1975.

Elber, Lynn. "Disaster Film Explosion Begins with 'Dante's Peak' Vocano Epic." The Associated Press. February 7, 1997.

Eldedge, Richard L. "Leoni Flick Has Stars and a Comet." The Atlanta Journal and Constitution. April 24, 1998.

Eller, Claudia. "Foreign Fare Has Hollywood Reviewing Strategy Abroad." Los Angeles Times. February 21, 1997.

Elliott, David. "Though Plot Twists are Few, 'Twister' Effects Hit Home." The San Diego Union-Tribune. May 10,1996.

English, Paul. "'Twister' Predicted to Hit City Theater Early in Storm Season." The Daily Oklahoman. Apil 23, 1996.

English, Paul. "Oklahoma Won't Flee Hollywood Twister." The Daily Oklahoman. March 31, 1995.

Evans, Gerald. "Fury as Film Men Break into Titanic." Evening Standard. October 3, 1995.

Faludi, Susan. "The Masculine Mistique; Film Star Sylvester Stallone." Esquire. December 1996.

Farber, Stephen. "'Jaws' and 'Bug' - The Only Difference is the Hype." The New York Times. August 24, 1975.

Feeney, Mary K. "Bugs Take Over the Movies: Is It Earth Next?." The Ottawa Citizen. September 2, 1997

Fleeman, Michael. "'Deep Impact' Shatters Expectations." Chicago Tribune. May 13m 1998.

Fleeman, Michael. "'Deep Impact' Tops 'Twister' Debut." AP Online. May 12, 1998.

Fleeman, Michael. "Another Asteroid Targets Film-Goers." AP Online. June 30, 1998.

Fleming, Michael. "The Backlot." Daily Variety. March 28, 1995.

Fleming, Michael. "Sly Sees 'Daylight.' Daily Variety. April 3, 1995.

Gabriel, Trip. "Post-Production Feels the Squeeze." International Herald Tribune. May 7, 1997.

Garner, Jack. "Hello Mimi Leder? Steven Spielberg Here, You're Ready for the Big Screen. Gannett News Service. September 23, 1997.

Gergart, Ann and Groer, Annie. "The Reliable Source." The Washington Post. July 16, 1997.

Giles, Jeff and Chang, Yahlin. "A Piece of the Action." Newsweek. June 9, 1997.

Goldstein, Patrick. "Hollywood's Endless Summer." Newsday. September 1, 1996.

Goodwin, Christopher. "Unsinkable Titanic?" Sunday Times. April 27, 1997.
Graustark, Barbara. "Newsmakers." Newsweek. December 18, 1978.

Gritten, David. "Back from the Abyss." Los Angeles Times. May 11, 1997.

Gromer, Cliff. "Delays at the Tunnel; Simulation of a Tunnel Explosion for the Sylvester Stallone Film 'Daylight'." Popular Mechanics. November, 1996.

Grove, Martin. "Zanuck's 'Impact' Hits After 22-Year Journey." The Hollywood Reporter. April 1, 1998.

Groves, Don. "O'Seas B.O Welcomes 'Daylight'." Variety. January 20, 1997.

Harris, Hamil R. "Getting in the Picture." The Washington Post. July 31, 1997.

Hartl, John. "Blowout or Fizzle Out?" The Seattle Times. April 24, 1997.

Heisler, Bob. "Like Jaws with a Rock in the Shark Role." Newsday. March 24, 1998.

Hoberman, J. "Apocalypse Now and Then." The Village Voice. May 19, 1998.

Hollinger, Hy. "ID4 Reign in Japan." The Hollywood Reporter. February 19, 1997.

Ivrym Bob. "At 50, Stallone Casts Himself in a Different Light." The Record. December 1, 1996.

Johnson, Reed. "Deeper Impact." Los Angeles Daily News. May 31, 1998.

Kaplan, Peter. "Michael Caine at 50 Testing the Limits of the Actor's Art." The New York Times. October 16, 1983.

Karlin, Susan. "Scott Ross: Digital Domain's CEO Launches a Studio by Sinking the Titanic." Upside. July 1998.

Karon, Paul. "Shell Game for 'Impact'." Daily Variety. July 21, 1997.

Kenyon, Tim. " 'Twister' Set to Spiral Over Area Within Days." Times Republican-

Marshalltown IA. July 20, 1995.

Ketcham, Diane. "Long Island Journal." The New York Times. August 10, 1997.

Kilday, Gregg and Thompson, Anne. "To Infinity and Below." Entertainment Weekly. February 2, 1996.

King, Susan. "Film Turkeys to Devour After Dinner." Los Angeles Times. November 27, 1997.

Kingsley, Barbara. "Star Watch: Rock Husdon Returns to the Movies." Associated Press. December 9, 1981.

Koncius, Jura. "Falling Starts." The Washington Post. August 9, 1978.

Kronke, David. "Disasters Just Waiting to Happen." Los Angeles Times. June 30, 1996.

Lewan, Todd. "The World is Safe: A Happy Ending to a One-day Asteroid Thriller." Associated Press. March 13, 1998.

Leys, Tony. "Hoping Fame Will Blow Their Way." The Des Moines Register. June 22, 1995.

Lippman, John. "A Direct Hit." The Wall Street Journal. March 17, 1998.

Longsdorf, Amy. "Top Guns; Heavyweights Dominate Upcoming Films." The Morning Call. August 30, 1996.

Lothery, Todd. "'Dante's Peak' Explodes On the Screen Successfully." The News and Observer. February 8, 1997.

Mack, Tara. "Extras Agree, They Oughta Be in Pictures." The Washington Post. July 16, 1997.

Martin, David M. "Kings of the World." Shoot. May 8, 1998.

Martin, Hugo. "Irwin Allen; 'Towering Inferno' Producer." Los Angeles Times. November 3, 1991.

Martin, Judith. " 'Meteor': Disasters From Many Star." The Washington Post. October 26, 1979.

Martin, Judith. "'Hurricane': Like Rain, Only Worse." The Washington Post. April 13, 1979.

Masters, Kim. "The Longest Day." Time. April 21, 1997.

Maxa, Rudy. "When Hollywood Came to Washington." The Washington Post. April 23, 1978.

McCarthy, Todd. "Daylight." Variety. December 2, 1996.

McDonald, Peter. "Titanic Film Set to Sing $200M." Evening Standard. April 18, 1997.

McDonald, Paula, "The $200-Million Return of the Titanic." The New York Times. April 5, 1997.

McDowell, Edwin. "Paul Gallico's Mine Still Yielding Gold." The New York Times. June 18, 1982.

McLellan, Joseph. "Disaster Revisited in

'Beyond Poseidon'." The Washington Post. August 4, 1979.

McNamara, Damian and Chang, Maria L. "Terror at the Movies." Science World. March 11, 1998.

McNary, Dave. "'Twister' Blows Away Field at U.S. Box Office." U.P.I. May 12, 1996.

McNutt, Michael. "Wakita Gets New Face for Movie Desctruction." The Sunday Oklahoman. April 23, 1995.

McNutt, Michael. "'Twister' Crew Enjoys Clear Sky." The Daily Oklahoman. May 25, 1995.

McNutt, Michael. "Early 'Twister' Fans Blowing Into Wakita." The Sunday Oklahoman. June 4, 1995.

Morgan, Gary. "Kate's Titanic Death Scare." The Mirror. April 21, 1997.

Murphy, Maggie. "Craze the 'Titanic'." Entertainment Weekly. September 13, 1996.

Myers, Randy. "These Films Were Intentional Disasters." The Dayton Daily News. May 16, 1996.

Myers, Randy. "A Disastrous Weekend, By George." The Dallas Morning News. May 11, 1996.

Newman, Bruce. "Call Her Cyclone Helen." Los Angeles Times. May 5, 1996.

Nichols, Peter M. "L.A. Out-Grimes New

York for Disaster Films." The Tampa Tribune. December 1, 1996.

Nusbaum, Eliot. "'Twister' Movie Cast, Crew Liked their Sushi." The Des Moines Register. August 26, 1995.

O'Donnell, Thomas. "Slater Not Slated for 'Twister' Scene's Movie Mayhem." The Des Moines Register. June 22, 1995.

O'Donnell, Thomas. "Whitten farmhouse gets ready for Role in 'Twister'." The Des Moines Register. July 7, 1995.

O'Donnell, Thomas. "Quiet Town Unfazed by Arrival of 'Twister'." The Des Moines Register. July 8, 1995.

O'Donnell, Thomas. "Movie Filming Mixes Glamour, Tedium." The Des Moines Register. August 3, 1995.

Oliver, Myrna. "Jennings Lang; Producer 'Airport' Movies." Los Angeles Times. May 31, 1996.

Orwall, Bruce and Lippman, John. "Movies Exploit Asteroid Scare." The Toronto Star. March 17, 1998.

O'Sullivan, Charlotte. "Disaster Prone." The Observer. July 14, 1996.

Parisi, Paula. "'Titanic' Film from Cameron Launched at Sea." The Hollywood Reporter. October 2, 1995.

Pearlman, Cindy. "Messing with Mother Nature." Chicago Sun-Times." February 2, 1997

Portman, Jamie. "Hunt Wanted No Part of Chasing Tornados: But Talk With Spielberg Convinced Her to Fit Role into Her Busy Schedule." The Ottawa Citizen. May 10, 1996.

Portman, Jamie. "Cameron's Next Film is a Titanic Project." The Vancouver Sun. February 23, 1996.

Price, Michael. "'Dante's Peak' Is Quite and Inferno." Fort Worth Star-Telegram." February 7, 1997.

Puig, Claudia. "Epic-Size Troubles on 'Titanic'." Los Angeles Times. April 19, 1997.

Puig, Claudia. "A Call to Industry to Reconsider Time Limits." Los Angeles Times. April 16, 1997.

Recer, Paul. "Experts Say There's a Small Chance of Large Asteroid Smashing Earth." Associated Press. March 12, 1998.

Reid, Alice. "Key Bridge to Close for Moviemakers." The Washington Post. July 16, 1997.

Remesch, Karin. "Extras Sought for Spielberg Production." The Sun. May 18, 1997.

Ryan, James. "Studios Entice Audiences With High-Tech Movie Web Sites." Chicago Tribune. November 15, 1996.

Sanello, Frank. "Razzie Awards Honor Worst Films, Stars of the Year." U.P.I. April 6, 1984.

Schaefer, Stephen. "'Twister' Puts Spin on High-Tech." The Boston Herald. May 5, 1996.

Schorow, Stephanie. "Cosmos of Chaos." The Boston Herald. January 29, 1997.

Scott, Vernon. "Sally Proves Versatility." U.P.I. December 21, 1982.

Seiler, Andy. "Floating a New Titanic Theory; Dramatic Iceberg Collision May Be Strictly Hollywood." USA Today. April 10, 1997.

Seiler, Andy. "The Sky is Falling." USA Today. May 7, 1998.

Setlowe, Richard. "Feats Falling Into Digital Safety Net." Variety. November 18, 1996.

Shales, Tom. "Film Notes." The Washington Post. July 14, 1978.

Shales, Tom. "Promomania." The Washington Post. July 23, 1978.

Shipman, David. "Obituary: Irwin Allen" The Independent. November. 4, 1991.

Shulgasser, Barbara. "'Twister'; It Blows Yard and Kicks Up a Lot of Dust – For What?" The San Francisco Examiner. May 10, 1996.

Smith, Liz. "Estee's New Face." Newsday. March 7, 1995.

Sommer, Constance. "Daring Celebrities Forgo Stuntmen." The Record. Oct. 14, 1996.

Staff. "Idaho Town Gets Only a Peek at 'Dante'." The Columbian. January 23, 1997.

Staff. "Cameron To Waive Some Fee." AP Online. May 5, 1997.

Staff. "July Preview." Entertainment Weekly. May 15, 1998.

Staff. "Dicaprio Sets Sail With Winslet." Reuters. May 22, 1996.

Staff. "Jennings Lang." Variety. June 9, 1996.

Staff. "Irwin Allen, 75, Master Producer of Disaster Pics, Dies." The Hollywood Reporter. November 4, 1991.

Staff. "Amazing Genius of Disaster Master." Sunday Mail. February 9, 1997.

Staff. "Rocky's Horror." Entertainment Weekly. December 20, 1996.

Staff. "Around Town." The Hollywood Reporter. February 16, 1995.

Staff. "Gertz, Elwes join 'Twister'." Daily Variety. April 5, 1995.

Staff. "A Watered-Down 'Aiport '77'." The Washington Post. March 25, 1977.

Staff. "Desperation in Hollywood: Actor Jack Lemmon's View." U.S. News and World Report. August 22, 1977.

Staff. "Funeral Services Set for Producer Irwin Allen." U.P.I. November 3, 1991.

Staff. "Australia Bans 'Skyjacked'" The New York Times. New York Times. August 9, 1972.

Staff. "When Time Ran Out." The Christina Science Monitor. April 11, 1980.

Staff. "Regional News" U.P.I. May 25, 1983.

Staff. "Recent Cases." Entertainment Law Reporter. October 1984.

Staff. "'Titanitc' Makes Hollywood Nervous." New York Times April 22, 1997.

Staff. "Movies; Try Surviving the Dialogue." Los Angeles Times. June 30, 1996.

Staff. "'Dante's' Producer Undaunted by Volcano Pic's Competition." October 27, 1996.

Staff. "William Castle, 63, Movie Producer." *The New York Times*. June 2, 1977.

Staff. "Obituaries, William Castle." Associated Press. June 2, 1977.

Staff. "Producer William Castle Dies at 63." *The Los Angeles Times*. June 3, 1977.

Staten, Vince. "Some Flood Movies Rise Above The Dull Gauge." The Courier-Journal. March 15, 1997.

Steyn, Mark. "The Arts: Just When You Thought It was Safe, The Disaster Movie Returns." The Daily Telegraph. July 25, 1996.

Strauss, Bob. "Dueling Volcanoes." The Daily News of Los Angeles. April 25, 1997.

Strauss, Bob. "Making Dreamworks Work."

The Boston Globe. September 21, 1997.

Stiefel, Chana Freiman. "Hollywood Erupts." Science World. February 7, 1997.

Stoynoff, Natasha. "A New Man." The Toronto Sun. December 1, 1996.

Sulski, Jim. "A Plague on the Land." Chicago Tribune. September 1, 1992.

Sutter, Ellie. "Movie Creates Building Boom in Guthrie Area." The Daily Oklahoman. July 21, 1995.

Svetkey, Benjamin. "Lava Is A Many-Splendored Thing." Entertainment Weekly. April 25, 1997.

Synnot, Siobhan. "13 Great Movie Disasters." Daily Record. January 23, 1998.

Thackerly Jr. Ted. "Rock Hudson Dies at59 After Fighting AIDS." Los Angeles Times. October 3, 1985.

Thomas, Bob. "Star Watch: Michael Caine Likes To Shake Up His Life." Associated Press. February 17, 1984.

Toner, Mike. "It's Coming, Earth: Cosmic Buckshot." The Atlanta Journal and Constitution. April 19, 1998.

Tookey, Christopher. "Spielberg Makes a Splash." Daily Mail. May 15, 1998.

Tookey, Christopher. "Why the Disaster Movie

Is Back with a Bang." Daily Mail. December 30, 1996.

Tran, Mark. "Titanic's Late Sailing Causes a Hollywood Traffic Jam." The Guardian. April 22, 1997.

Treleven, Ed. "Tornado Chasers Live for Darkening Skies." Wisconsin State Journal. April 10, 1996.

Turan, Kenneth. "Magma Opus." Times News Service. February 7, 1997.

Turan, Kenneth. "The Big Spin." Los Angeles Times. May 10, 1996.

Vlessing, Etan. "Sinking Feeling: PCP on 'Titanic'." BPI Entertainment News Wire. August 29, 1996

Vosburgh, Dick. "Obituary: Jennings Lang." The Independent. June 13, 1996.

Weeks, Janet. "Hollywood Taking a Winter Gamble." Los Angeles Daily News. January 30, 1997.

Weeks, Janet. "U.S. Film Rules Over Foreign Box Office." Daily News of Los Angeles. May 12, 1997.

Weiner, Rex and Busch, Anita. "MGM Insures Future." Variety. January 27, 1997.

Weintraub, Bernard. "Hollywood Braces for Likely Delay of 'Titanic'." New York Times. April 21, 1997.

Westbrook, Bruce. "Can 'Twister' Churn Up

187

Some Stars?" The Houston Chronicle. May 5, 1996.

Westbrook, Bruce. "Charlton Heston Back in the Drivers Seat." The Houston Chronicle. February 23, 1992.

Williams, Jeannie. "Stallone Ready For Women of Action." USA Today. October 15, 1996.

Wirt, John. "Armageddon's Impact Numbs Rather Than Thrills." The Advocate. July 10, 1998.

Woods, Mark. "Quartet Heads for $100 Million Overseas." Variety. October 20, 1997.

Wyrick, Wayne. "Disaster Films Don't Show Deep Impact." The Sunday Oklahoman. August 2, 1998.

Young, Deborah. "Stallone Sees 'Daylight,' Has Sites Set on Cinecitta." Variety. Jun 4, 1995.

Zito, Tom. "'The Swarm': It's the Real Sting." The Washington Post. July 15, 1978.

index

Symbols

101 Dalmations 139

A

ABC Network Television 62
Abyss, The 125
Academy Award 23
Affleck, Ben 170
Airforce One 83
Airplane 19
Airport 13
Airport 75 45
Airport '77 81
Airport '80: The Concorde 81
Airport 1979 81
Airport 2000 82
Akins, Claude 78
Albert, Eddie 82
Albertson, Jack 39
Aliens 144
Allen, Irwin 13
All I Desire 32
All My Children 70
American International Pictures 103
Anderson, Bibi 82
Andrews, Dana 79
Andromeda Strain, The 127
A Night to Remember 155
Animal World, The 38
A Place in the Sun 39
Arkoff, Samuel Z. 104
Armageddon 15
Armstong, Jerome 151
Astaire, Fred 19
Asteroid 149
Atlantis, the Lost Continent 24
Avalanche 45

B

Bachelor Father 55
Backstreet 32
Bad Seed, The 70
Ball, Lucille 31
Bantam Books 62
Bates, Kathy 157
Bay, Michael 170

Bedelia, Bonnie 83
Beginning of the End, The 23
Bellwood, Pamela 80
Benchley, Peter 62
Ben Hur 77
Beyond The Poseidon Adventure 99
Big Circus, The 38
Birds, The 15
Birth of a Nation 20
Bisset, Jacqueline 32
Black, Karen 79
Blair, Linda 79
Blakely, Susan 46
Blazing Saddles 79
Blob, The 23
Bloom, Claire 137
Bohem, Leslie 135
Bolden, Elizabeth 158
Bonnie and Clyde 39
Borgnine, Ernest 39
Bottoms, Timothy 57
Boxoffice 90
Boyle, Peter 100
Brady Bunch, The 47
Brenneman, Amy 137
Bridges, Jeff 83
Broken Arrow 127
Brolin, James 78
Brosnan, Pierce 143
Brown, David 164
Bruckheimer, Jerry 171
Bug 15, 65
Bujold, Genevieve 56
Burgess, Don 129
Burton, Richard 38
Buscemi, Steve 170
Buttons, Red 39

C

Cadillac Man 144
Caesar, Sid 79
Caine, Michael 19, 87
Calamity Jane 114
Cameron, James 155
Capricorn One 79
Carrera, Barbara 115
Cartwright, Angela 100

About the Author

John William Law is an editor and journalist whose work has appeared in newspapers, magazines and books. In all, he has worked on the staffs of six daily, three weekly and several monthly publications. He has also been the editor, writer and research of a number of books by other authors. As a freelance writer his work has appeared in magazines and in print and he has been interviewed for print, television and radio programs about ilm history and the entertainment industry. His books include *Curse of the Silver Screen - Tragedy & Disaster Behind the Movies (1999)*, *Reel Horror - True Horrors Behind Hollywood's Scary Movies (2004)*, *Master of Disaster: Irwin Allen (2008)* and *Alfred Hitchcock: The Icon Years (2010)*.

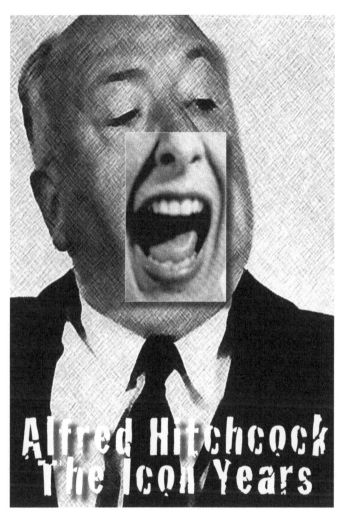

If you enjoyed this title you might also like "Alfred Hitchcock: The Icon Years," also from Aplomb Publishing. The book takes readers behind the scenes of the Master of Suspense's films at the peak of his career. With rare photos and behind-the-scenes talks of motion picture history, films include Psycho, The Birds, Marnie, Torn Curtain, Frenzy, Family Plot and more. Available in print and ebook.

Lightning Source UK Ltd.
Milton Keynes UK
UKOW06f2244171114

241765UK00009B/535/P